LETTER TO A ONE L FRIEND

LETTER TO A ONE L FRIEND

A LITTLE GUIDE TO SEEING THE BIG PICTURE
AND SUCCEEDING IN LAW SCHOOL

Isaac Mamaysky

CAROLINA ACADEMIC PRESS

Durham, North Carolina

ISBN   978-1-5310-1103-1
e-ISBN   978-1-5310-1104-8

Library of Congress Cataloging-in-Publication Data
Names: Mamaysky, Isaac, author.
Title: Letter to a one L friend : a little guide to seeing the big picture
    and succeeding in law school / by Isaac Mamaysky.
Description: Durham, North Carolina : Carolina Academic Press, LLC, [2019]
    | Includes bibliographical references.
Identifiers: LCCN 2019003155 | ISBN 9781531011031 (alk. paper)
Subjects: LCSH: Law--Study and teaching--United States--Handbooks, manuals,
    etc. | Law students--United States--Handbooks, manuals, etc. |
    Law--Anecdotes.
Classification: LCC KF283 .M36 2019 | DDC 340.071/173--dc23
LC record available at https://lccn.loc.gov/2019003155

Carolina Academic Press
700 Kent Street
Durham, North Carolina 27701
Telephone (919) 489-7486
Fax (919) 493-5668
www.cap-press.com
Printed in the United States of America

To Lisa, Eve, and Levi

"When one has finished building one's house, one suddenly realizes that in the process one has learned something that one really needed to know in the worst way—before one began."

-Friedrich Nietzsche

CONTENTS

ACKNOWLEDGMENTS

This book was born out of a letter I wrote to a friend who was just starting law school. Perhaps I felt compelled to help him out of a debt of gratitude to the countless people who helped me.

Lisa, thank you for your love, partnership, encouragement, and insightful editing. In this project and everything else in life, your support means so much to me. Eve and Levi, thank you for bringing so much joy into our lives. If you ever decide to attend law school, perhaps this book might be helpful.

Mom and dad, your faith in me is the foundation of anything I might accomplish. Your work ethic, dedication, and resilience are an example to the younger members of our family. Thank you for being amazing parents and grandparents.

Rosalie, Lester (Z"L), and Mara, thank you for making our individual aspirations into family projects. And thank you for so frequently and lovingly watching the babies (and dog), and thus creating a window to pursue projects like this.

Kelly and Harry, remember those letters of advice you wrote when I started college? I loved reading them, and they were always in the back of my mind while writing this book. Thank you for being the best brother and sister-in-law anybody could ask for. Sasha, Talia, and Liv, thank you for making everything brighter and being amazing role models for Eve and Levi.

Cheryl, thank you for inspiring me and so many of your former students, and empowering us to live better lives using the tools of philosophy. The world needs more teachers like you.

Professor Farnsworth, your Civil Procedure midterm was my first exam. After submitting my answers, I spent a couple weeks questioning whether I was cut out for law school. And then I received my grade. Your kindness put the wind back in my sails, and I remain grateful after all these years.

Wentworth Miller, I attended your LEEWS workshop towards the end of first semester. Those few hours transformed my approach to law school, and I'm sure some of your lessons have made their way into this book. I recommend your course to all my readers.

Alon, Dani, Jacob (a classmate in spirit), Karim, Katie, Pete, Rishab, Stacey, and Vikas, when I think back to our lunches in the faculty dining room, nights at Cornwall's, epic ski trips, coffee-fueled study sessions, and pure joy celebrating the end of finals, it always brings a big smile to my face. I look back warmly on law school because of your friendship. As Katie used to shout before each exam, "Good luck everyone!"

Cousin David, Elliot, Laurie, and Rachel, I am proud that you are my coworkers and friends. You are the best team anyone could ask for. Your talented management and deep care for our work allow me to spend time on projects like this. I am so grateful for all of you.

Karim, thank you for patiently editing this book, multiple times, and enthusiastically agreeing to write the foreword. Your influence is felt throughout.

Finally, Carol McGeehan, Kathleen Soriano Taylor, and the entire staff of Carolina Academic Press, thank you for making this project a reality.

PREFACE

I wrote this book with one goal: to teach you how to earn high grades in law school. I tried to make it a quick, easy read that you can finish in a few hours and then reference as needed during 1L year and beyond.

As you may have already discovered, many books on this topic are much longer and broader in scope. Often written by brilliant, well-intentioned professors who have long forgotten what it's like to be students, they include chapters on who should attend law school, the lawyer's impact on society, and conflicting theories of legal reasoning. While these are certainly interesting and valuable topics, I wanted *Letter to a 1L Friend* to be different, and much shorter.

In my final year of law school, an attorney friend advised me to read *The Curmudgeon's Guide to Practicing Law*. The book is punchy, humorous, full of anecdotes, and exactly what every new associate needs to know but nobody tells them. I read the whole thing in a couple hours and referenced it throughout my first few years of practice. I kept thinking, *this is the kind of book new law students need*. And then I wrote *Letter to a 1L Friend*.

After reading this short guide, my goal is for you to arrive on the first day of school ready to hit the ground running. You'll know exactly what to expect and exactly what to do to rise to the very top of your class. I wish you the best of luck.

Isaac Mamaysky
Rye, NY

"Assumpsit" was the first word that I read in law school.

I was a new law student and had just started my reading assignment for contracts, one of the required first year classes. The assignment involved reading several ancient legal cases in a textbook creatively titled "Contracts." In fact, the textbook itself looked like it could have been as old as the cases. It reproduced each case, one after another, with little in the way of context or guidance. It was the first case in that Contracts casebook that began with a one-word sentence: "Assumpsit."

I dutifully looked up the word in my legal dictionary, typed the definition into my notes, and continued reading, often stopping to look up unfamiliar words and reread confusing passages. The reading assignment took much longer than expected, but by the end of the night, I felt reasonably sure that I understood what happened in all the cases. "That wasn't too bad," I thought to myself.

The next day in class, however, I quickly learned that our professor was less interested in the details of each case and more interested in the legal principle, or what each case meant about the law. As the semester went on, I would also learn that he expected us to understand how the cases fit together.

Two cases that seemed particularly mysterious, at least to us first-year law students, illustrate this point well. One involved a dispute about ownership of a goat, the other a cow. The facts were almost identical. The lawyers made similar arguments. And the cases took place in the same timeframe and jurisdiction. Yet, in one case the plaintiff won and in the other case the defendant won. We struggled with those cases, trying to figure out why. Could it be that there were different laws for goats and cows?

Eventually we understood that the key difference was simply who had physical possession of the animal at the beginning of the lawsuit. From there followed the simple principle that courts do not like to interfere in personal matters. That principle became actionable knowledge that we could apply to exam questions.

All law students encounter challenges, and you will inevitably struggle through difficult material. But certain rules, such as focusing on the principle of each case, will ensure you study most effectively. Once law school starts, you won't have time to focus on *how* to study; keeping up with the substance of each class will be challenging enough on its own. That's why you should formulate your strategy *before* law school starts. This book will show you how.

Isaac has great insight about what it takes to succeed in law school. Not only did he graduate with top grades and multiple academic honors, but Isaac has always taken an interest in helping students excel. In law school, he mentored 1Ls and taught them the proven strategy you're about to read. He ultimately wrote a letter of all his advice to a close friend who was just getting started. I am glad that Isaac turned his letter into a book because it enables every aspiring law student to benefit from his mentorship. I have no doubt that this advice will serve you well, whether or not you understand your first reading assignment.

Karim Z. Oussayef, Esq.
Partner, Desmarais LLP

LETTER TO A ONE L FRIEND

TRIAL BY FIRE

On one of the first nights of law school orientation, I found myself at a bar with my future classmates. After a few drinks and some mildly inappropriate stories from undergrad, I established a rapport with a classmate and confided in her that I was pretty nervous about law school. "After all," I explained, "it seems like everyone here was a star in college, but since there's a curve now, only a few of us can stand out."

My new friend confided in me too. "In college I never worked that hard, but I did really well. I didn't even prepare my thesis presentation, and I was hungover, but I got a standing ovation! I also graduated fifth in my high school class. To be honest, I didn't work much back then either. So really, I'm just not that concerned about law school."

Fall semester seemed to fly by. Just a few months later, our first final exam was over and I once again found myself at a bar with these same people—by now good friends. This time, however, the mood was completely different. After a few drinks, my friend (the one who never really worked that hard in college) was in tears. "Never mind not understanding the first two questions on that Torts exam," she sobbed, "I didn't even *answer* the last question."

And so it goes with law school: Bright, successful students come in, thinking the world of their abilities, and law school breaks them. I was almost one of these students. Having started 1L year with no clear plan or strategy, I was disappointed to end first semester with an unimpressive performance. Thankfully, I figured out the right process before it was too late and graduated in a very different position.

Like most new law students, I didn't realize that hard work and intelligence aren't enough to succeed. Many of your classmates will study during every waking moment just to stay in the middle of the pack. This is because law school requires a unique method of analysis, completely different from anything you did in undergrad. Despite what many students think, doing well is more about process than intelligence. Students who use the correct process excel, while students who use the wrong process don't—regardless of how smart they are. Having a clear strategy when you begin law school is almost as important as working hard once you get there.

You've picked a good place to start. This book was born out of a letter I wrote as a 3L to a good friend who was just starting his first year. Since I wrote most of this book as a student, the bewilderment of 1L year and the stress of exams were still tangible. I took the time to put my advice on paper purely as a labor of love so my friend would enjoy his first year more than I did. I'd like to think this letter made things a little easier for him, and I hope it will do the same for you.

Key Points

- Law school requires a unique method of analysis, completely different from anything you did in undergrad.
- To excel, you need the right strategy and process, and that's what this book will teach you.

CHAPTER ONE

THE PARABLE OF THE OVERLY ZEALOUS LAW STUDENT

On the first day of law school, one of my favorite professors told the following story: Once upon a time, a dedicated law student was studying for her hardest exam. Following a semester of thoughtful reading and enthusiastic class participation, her notes were about 100 pages long. She began preparing for exams by simplifying these 100 pages to make a 25-page outline.

After learning the 25 pages inside out and backwards, she kept shortening her outline until it was a 1-page summary of the entire course. Despite all her efforts, the dedicated law student was besieged with worry on the night before the exam. She decided the only thing to do was stay up all night and turn her once-100 pages of notes into a single word. Unfortunately, on the day of the exam, she forgot the word!

The joke and lesson of this memorable (albeit cheesy) story is this: If you study by grappling with, refining, and simplifying your book notes and class notes, then there's no way you can forget the material.

The student in the story mostly got it right. Aside from turning the outline into a single word, her process is the one you should follow to prepare for exams. Specifically, you should do two things for each class: (1) take the mass of information you accumulate all semester and turn it into a concise 25-page outline; and (2) turn your 25-page outline into a 1-page summary of the entire class.

The advice below will elaborate on these goals and explain how to achieve them.

Key Points

- You should do two things for each class:
    - (1) Take the mass of information you accumulate all semester and turn it into a concise 25-page outline; and
    - (2) Turn your 25-page outline into a 1-page summary of the entire class.
- The pages that follow will unpack these goals.

CHAPTER TWO

THE JOY OF CASEBOOKS

In each class, you'll have one casebook with all the reading for the entire semester. All casebooks are organized the same way: They consist of cases followed by notes and hypothetical questions about the cases. Before getting to the correct approach to both types of reading, let's discuss why it's important to keep your reading notes brief.

A. A LENGTHY DISCUSSION ON THE VALUE OF BREVITY

During my last year of law school, I was an advisor to a few first-year students. After the second week of school, I met with one of my advisees to take a look at her notes and give her some tips about exam preparation. I asked whether she found the reading hard. "To be honest, it's terrible," she said. "I don't know how everyone does it. I spend hours and hours reading my cases but don't really get the point." She went on to tell me her process. "First, I just read the case. Then, I read the case again and use highlighters to identify the important points. After that, I read the case a third time and type up the highlighted points." Upon further investigation, I discovered that each of her case summaries took up an entire single-spaced page in Microsoft Word. That's the *wrong* way to do things.

To excel in law school, you should learn to read large homework assignments quickly and then summarize those homework assignments in a few short paragraphs. The reasons for this are twofold: (1) the faster you finish your reading, the more time you'll have to review old material; and (2) the shorter your reading notes, the less old material you'll have to review.

Keep in mind, professors assign reading until the last day of classes. Over the course of first semester, you'll read roughly 600 pages in each class. You won't have much time to review old material because you'll have to keep up with new assignments. Moreover, once classes end your final exams will be spaced three or four days apart, which doesn't leave much time to prepare. In light of these time constraints, you should read quickly and keep your reading notes brief.

In most first year classes, you'll have no more than 20 pages of reading per class. If you follow the advice below, reading and taking a few paragraphs of notes on a 20-page assignment should take two highly focused and productive hours.[1] After a while, you'll realize that the ten-page readings assigned when law school first started were a walk in the park.

B. READING CASES

Your homework assignments and class discussions will center on the cases in your casebook. As discussed below, how you read and summarize those cases is very important.

1. Writing Briefs

Successful students summarize the cases assigned for homework in short write-ups which are appropriately called "briefs." If you've never seen a case, take a look at Appendix A. The traditional brief—the kind they teach you to make during law school orientation—answers the following questions in a few short sentences:

---

1. On the off-chance you have a professor who gives longer reading assignments, it's better to stay current than maintain the ratio of ten pages per hour. As discussed in more detail below, it also becomes much more important to take meticulous notes during class.

- **Facts:** What are the facts of the case?
    - Don't focus on the details. Instead, tell the *story of the case* or explain the *point of the facts*.
- **Issue:** What legal question does the court answer? In other words, what is the issue?
    - Consider the chapter of your book and section of your syllabus in which the case appears. The legal question always relates to that subject.
- **Procedural Posture:** What happened in the lower court?
    - Many law school cases are appeals of lower court decisions.
- **Resolution:** How did the court decide the dispute between the parties?
- **Holding:** How did the court resolve the issue/legal question? In other words, what is the "rule of law?"
- **Rationale:** What was the court's reasoning?

2. A Briefer Brief

In the notes you take while reading homework assignments, you can use the traditional style of brief explained above. In your exam outlines, discussed a little later, you should condense the traditional brief into a few sentences which answer the following questions:

- **Facts:** What are the facts?
- **Issue:** What is the legal question?
- **Holding:** How does the court answer that question?
- **Rationale:** Why does the court answer that way?

3. Practice

Try writing a full brief of the case in Appendix A. Even though the case is long, you should make your brief as short as possible. Once you're done, take a look at the brief below. Note that this is the traditional style of brief used to prepare for class, rather than the shorter style you would use on an exam outline.

Hammontree v. Jenner (California Appeals Court, 1971)

- **Facts:** A man prone to seizures had a seizure while driving and injured the plaintiff.
- **Issue:** Does the theory of "absolute liability"[2] apply to a driver who has a seizure while driving?
- **Procedural Posture:** Lower court held that absolute liability does not apply and appeals court affirmed.
- **Resolution:** Court held that driver was not liable because he took medicine to prevent seizures and doctors told him it was safe to drive.
- **Holding:** Absolute liability does not apply to drivers who are prone to seizures but take preventative steps and receive a doctor's permission to drive. Drivers are only liable if they acted negligently.
- **Rationale:** Imposing absolute liability on drivers would complicate the law of automobile accidents and should only be imposed by the legislature.

For another example, try briefing the case in Appendix B. You can compare your work to the brief below.

Shapira v. Union National Bank (Ohio, 1974)

- **Facts:** Father's will said: My son only gets a gift if he marries a woman of a certain religion. Son sues to invalidate this condition.
- **Issue:** Can a will condition a gift on the religion of the recipient's future spouse?
- **Procedural Posture:** This is a lower court decision.
- **Resolution:** The court upheld the condition.
- **Holding:** A gift in a will can be conditioned on the religion of the recipient's future spouse.

---

2. "Absolutely liability" means the driver is liable regardless of the specific facts of the case. For example, some states impose absolute liability on drunk drivers. They're liable even if the accident wasn't technically their fault.

- **Rationale:** The condition is not an unconstitutional restriction on marriage. It is merely a restriction on the receipt of a gift. Also, the condition does not violate public policy because it is only a partial (rather than complete) restriction on marriage and it is not a restriction of the son's freedom of religion. Finally, it is reasonable for a person to use his will to further the interests of a religious group.

C. PICKING NEEDLES OUT OF A HAYSTACK

Many new law students find it difficult — as they should — to summarize a 10- or 15-page case in a few short sentences. However, this is essential to doing well in law school. Although you'll read about 600 pages per class, you must walk into each final exam with a 25-page outline — an impossible task if your briefs are any longer than a few sentences.

On final exams, you'll need to know the principle of each case rather than the details. For example, *Hammontree* stands for the principle that drivers are only liable for accidents if they acted negligently. You need to know the details of the case just well enough to speak intelligently about that principle.

As you might have gathered from *Hammontree* and *Shapira*, courts make many statements about the law. You should not include all these statements in your briefs. Each case appears in your casebook because of how the court resolved *one* issue. Your goal is to identify that issue and its resolution. If you focus only on the statements of law concerning the issue, then you will understand the point of the case and your briefs will stay concise. To help identify the issue, check your syllabus and the book's table of contents before reading the case. The legal issue will always relate to the subject noted in those materials.

Let's assume you've been assigned a case in Contracts class. Prior to looking at the case, you check your syllabus and see that the reading comes under the heading "How to Make a Binding Contract." Next, you check the casebook's table of contents and discover that the case appears in the chapter entitled "Making Contracts."

Before you've even seen the case, you know that the relevant, brief-worthy legal statements have something to do with how to make a contract. Although the court spends two pages discussing the law of ending contracts, you don't include anything from those two pages in your brief. Likewise, although the court spends a paragraph discussing the relevant standard to grant a "motion to dismiss" (whatever that is!), you don't include that discussion in your brief either—it has nothing to do with the law of forming contracts.

A common beginner's mistake is noting every legal statement a court makes. This is why you'll sometimes see 1L classmates highlight nearly every line of a case! If a Contracts case appears in a chapter about making contracts, they'll take notes on the court's statements about the motion to dismiss. A few months into law school, they *might* realize that motions to dismiss are covered in another class called Civil Procedure, in a chapter of the casebook appropriately called "Motions to Dismiss."

By the time you go through a semester or two of law school, picking out the relevant parts of your cases will come as second nature. Eventually, you'll take very short reading notes at home *and* find that your professors aren't telling you anything new during class. At the beginning, however, picking out the relevant parts of a case will be hard. Keeping your reading notes concise may mean that you occasionally (or more than occasionally) miss an important point. That's okay. Your professors will cover everything important about a case during class, so any point you miss while briefing will end up in your outline anyway.[3] At the beginning, when it's still a struggle to determine what's relevant, try to avoid the temptation to write

---

3. This is also why you should never spend hours and hours trying to understand a case. Most of your time should be dedicated to outlining (*i.e.*, reviewing and studying your book notes and class notes), as we'll discuss in more detail below.

down everything. If you focus on the *one* reason each case is in your book and disregard extraneous legal statements, your briefs will stay *brief* and you'll understand the point of each case. With all this in mind, if you want to try briefing an especially long and complicated case, see *Dodge v. Ford Motor Company* in Appendix C.

D. THE "NOTES AND QUESTIONS" SECTION

When law school first started, I frequently pulled all-nighters because the reading took so long. This was a big mistake—you should never pull an all-nighter in law school. During your first year, you can safely expect to sleep eight hours a night, go to the gym six days a week, and even go out once in a while.

So where did I go wrong? Aside from taking too much time to read and brief cases, I took too long to read the notes and questions sections following the cases. To be "thorough," I went so far as to *answer* the hypothetical questions in writing, wasting precious time that I should have spent reviewing my class notes and making sense of my outline.

To avoid my time-consuming mistake, you should skim the notes and questions sections. Concentrate on the theme of each note, rather than the details. If you're unsure whether a point is important, leave it out of your outline. If it *is* important, your professor will go over it during class, so it will end up in your outline anyway.

What kinds of points in the notes and questions sections are relevant? These include any statement of the law (*e.g.*, "the majority of courts hold..."), a summary of the important holdings in a complicated case, or an abridged case. In contrast, the hypothetical questions, a list of statutes from 15 different jurisdictions, an exposition on the history of tort law, or an excerpt from the likes of Locke, Hobbes, or Kant are completely irrelevant to exams.[4]

---

4. Your professors' hypotheticals, which will be posed to students in class, are much more important than the hypotheticals in the book. They will give you in-

I can't give you a complete list of the things you shouldn't take notes on, but keep the following in mind for guidance: When you sit down for a final exam, you need to know *the law*—in other words, how the majority of jurisdictions would resolve the issue which landed each case in the book. In the absence of a clear majority, you will need to know the primary competing views. You will never need to know a flowery, academic theory about the origin of laws.

E. CONCLUSION: ERR ON THE SIDE OF EXCLUSION WHEN READING

Remember that your overarching goal is to turn 600 pages of reading and 50 hours of class into a 25-page outline. The most important skill in law school is the ability to condense 20 pages of casebook reading into a few short bullet points. At the beginning, you won't know which parts of your reading are relevant and which parts are irrelevant, so you'll be tempted to take over-inclusive notes.

Just keep in mind, the brevity of your outline is far more important than any substantive law you might leave out by taking short notes. When in doubt, err on the side of exclusion. Your professors will flag the most important points during class, so even if you miss them while reading, they will end up in your outline anyway. As discussed in the next chapter, this is why you should err on the side of *inclusion* while taking class notes.

Key Points

- You'll read about 600 pages per class, but you need to walk into the final exam with a 25-page outline. This is impossible if your reading notes are more than a few sentences.
- On final exams, you'll need to know the principle of each case rather than the details. Each case appears in your

---

sight into the questions on the final exam and, more abstractly, teach you how to reason about the law.

book because of how the court resolved one legal issue. To keep your briefs to a few sentences and understand the point of each case, focus only on that issue and resist the temptation to write down everything the court says about the law.

- The headings in your casebook and syllabus shed light on the issue in each case, so check the headings before you start reading.
- It's okay if you miss an important point when taking notes on the reading. Your professors will cover everything important during class, so the key points will end up in your outline anyway.
- Skim the Notes and Questions sections, but always take notes on any statement of the law ("the majority of courts hold..."), summary of an important case, or abridged case.

CHAPTER THREE

MAKING THE MOST OF CLASS TIME

A. THE SOCRATIC METHOD

Most of your professors will be very nice. They'll try to make class enjoyable and work hard to ensure the material is totally understandable. Of all the professors at my law school, I can only name one exception to this rule.

We had a professor who was notorious for mistreating students. He failed 1Ls even though the curve didn't require it, assigned a hundred pages of reading per class, and maintained a website singing his own praises. In one often-told story, Professor "Smith" randomly called on a 1L to answer questions about the prior night's reading. Apparently not satisfied with her answers, Smith asked the student to read her notes aloud to the entire class. He proceeded to pose a series of specific questions about why certain points were included while others were not, and only let up once the student was in tears.

That student was "on call" and Professor Smith was practicing an especially pernicious version of the "Socratic Method."[5] Many new students mistakenly think this type of thing is normal in law

---

5. Socrates believed that before people are born their souls are exposed to absolute truth. According to Socrates, people forget this truth upon birth but can be reminded of it by a teacher who asks the right questions. Luckily, your professors have more modest goals.

school. They imagine 100-page readings, mean professors, and intimidating classes. That couldn't be further from the truth! Your professors will be nice, they'll assign reasonable homework assignments (usually about 20 pages per class), and they'll be understanding when students are on call.

I don't tell the story of Smith to scare you, but rather to make the following point: He was such an exception to the rule that when he left for another law school, our comedy group performed a five minute song called "Professor Smith is a Giant...." Well, I'll leave the rest to your imagination. That sketch resulted in a standing ovation from professors and students alike. His behavior isn't what the community values, and you won't have a Smith at your law school.

In first year classes, professors will call on you to answer questions about the prior night's reading. Unlike Smith, they'll be pretty cool about it. Some professors ask straightforward questions regarding the basic facts and main issues in the cases assigned for homework. Others ask more theoretical questions, such as how a court's reasoning might apply to a different set of facts. Let's take the case we discussed a few pages ago, *Hammontree v. Jenner*, as an example:

Professor: What if the driver of the car didn't know he was prone to seizures? How would the court have ruled then?

Student: The same way. The driver wouldn't have been liable. In Hammontree, the court didn't impose liability because doctors told the driver it was safe to drive, and the driver modified his behavior to reduce the likelihood of a seizure. That was enough to avoid liability. If a person doesn't know that he might have a seizure, a court can't expect him to modify his behavior.

Professor: Good response, but let me follow up: What about the people he injured? Is it any consolation to them that the driver didn't know he would have a seizure? Aren't they innocent too?

Aside from demonstrating the legal reasoning process, such exchanges illuminate how to think through questions on final exams. Being on call only feels scary because it involves speaking in front of such a large audience. The questions will either be simple, so you'll know the answers, or they won't have a right or wrong answer, so you can't get them wrong. Also, keep in mind that many professors allow students to "drop a note"—once or twice a semester, you can leave a note on the professor's desk asking not to be on call that day.

1. Read Casebooks to Prepare for Exams, Not for Class

Now that we've spoken a little about class, let's add some color to our earlier discussion about keeping your reading notes brief. On exams, you will need to know the principle of each case. While reading, you should focus on how the court resolves the one legal issue that landed each case in the book.

During class discussions, professors ask hypothetical questions to help you learn to reason about the law. Using those questions, professors fill gaps in the briefs you made at home and eventually draw out the principle of each case; and that's the part you'll need in your outline for final exams.

Here's the key point: Your job as a law student is to prepare for exams rather than class. Many students take extensive notes on their reading so they feel ready to answer their professors' hypotheticals. That just wastes precious time that they should spend outlining and preparing for exams. Keep in mind, a masterful performance on call won't do anything to raise your exam grade. Indeed, many of the most talkative students become very quiet after the first set of grades comes out.

So keep your eye on the prize—doing well on exams—and don't spend extra time reading so you feel prepared for every potential hypothetical. You should prepare for class the exact same way you prepare for exams: by briefing your cases in a few sentences and taking very short notes on the rest of your reading. This will ensure that you have the most possible time to review your class notes and synthesize them with your book notes after each class (a concept that we'll discuss in more detail below).

B. CLASS NOTES

1. The Internet Distraction

If you have the discipline to make good use of your class time, it will pay off immensely at the end of the semester. Like the rest of your classmates, you'll likely take notes on a laptop during class. While very convenient, this means you'll have internet access, which can be a huge distraction.

I predict that roughly a third of your classmates will spend most of class sending texts and e-mails, another third will shop online or waste time on social media, and one or two might even watch television shows on silent, as one of my classmates was known to do during Property class (which was especially strange because he sat in the front row, so everyone could see his screen!). Taking good class notes is crucial to doing well on exams, and it's a simple way to gain an edge over many of your classmates. Dare I say, you might want to turn off your phone and keep your computer offline during class.

2. Err on the Side of Inclusion During Class

As discussed above, when law school starts, you'll be unable to distinguish the relevant from the irrelevant, both in your reading and during class. In the interest of time, you should adopt a presumption of irrelevance when it comes to taking notes on the reading—if you're not sure whether to include something in your outline, err on the side of exclusion. You can safely make this presumption while reading because you make the exact opposite presumption during class, where you err on the side of *inclusion* and write down everything your professor says. While outlining after class, you can synthesize your class notes and reading notes and, after calm deliberation, delete irrelevant points. We'll discuss how to outline in the next chapter.

Key Points

- Professors randomly call on students to answer questions about the reading. Don't spend extra time on reading assignments so you feel prepared for your professors' hypotheticals. Your goal while reading is to prepare for exams by briefing cases in a few sentences and taking short notes on the rest of your reading.
- Stay offline during class. Taking meticulous class notes is crucial to doing well on exams, and it's a simple way to gain an edge over your classmates.
- If you're unsure if a point is relevant while reading, then leave it out of your notes. If you're unsure if a point is relevant during class, then put it in your notes.
- While outlining after each class, you'll synthesize your class notes and book notes, and determine what portions of the class notes to delete.

CHAPTER FOUR

THE BIG PICTURE AND THE IMPORTANCE OF OUTLINING

When I was still in college, an accomplished lawyer told me the story of her highest 1L grade. Just before finals week, she was reading her torts outline while riding the subway to school. In her words, "the big picture suddenly clicked," and she felt completely prepared for the exam.

Over time, I heard the same sentiment from professors, lawyers, and high-performing upperclassmen. They would say things like, "Focus on the big picture," "Make sure to see the forest from the trees," and "Don't get caught up in the weeds." Perhaps you've heard this advice too. If you're anything like me, you were left wondering what it means: *How do I see the big picture? What should I do?* In this chapter, I'm going to demystify the concept and teach you exactly how to see the big picture before every final exam.

A. WHAT IS THE BIG PICTURE?

Think back to your first day of college. The campus seemed huge, right? You probably started by looking over the campus map. By the time you settled into the dorm and your parents left, you found the dining hall, and by the second day of orientation, you knew which buildings your classes were in. As the weeks turned into months, you learned more and more of the campus until, eventually, it didn't seem so big after all.

Outlining a class is surprisingly similar. At first, all you have is a thick casebook about a subject you've barely heard of — the class seems overwhelming. You start by studying your maps — the class' syllabus and the casebook's table of contents. Keeping the different sections of class in mind, you go on to learn a bunch of details about individual cases. By the end of the semester, you allow the details to fade into the background while focusing on how the different sections of class connect.

Once you understand and memorize the legal principle of each case, how the case fits into its section of class, and how the different sections of class connect, you will "see" the big picture. When that happens, you'll be completely prepared for the final exam. To make sure it happens, you should outline all semester, starting from day one.

B. HOW TO OUTLINE

Let's begin by recapping what we've already covered: Before class, you should summarize the cases assigned for homework and take brief notes on the reading. During class, you should pay close attention and write down almost everything your professor says. Right after class, while the material is fresh, you should spend 45 minutes "outlining," by shortening your class notes and synthesizing them with your book notes while focusing on the principle of each case.[6]

By the last day of class, you should have gone through your book notes and class notes at least once. This will leave you with a roughly 100-page outline going into reading week and finals period. I assume that you won't have enough time during the semester to go through your book notes and class notes more than once. However, if you *can* go through your notes more than once, your outline will be shorter than 100 pages, and in turn, the process described below will be easier.

---

6. To make outlining easier, you can keep all your notes in one Word document. Take class notes in blue, directly under your book notes, which should be in black.

Assuming you have a 100-page outline on the last day of class, your next step is to cut out unnecessary details and make a 75-page outline, then a 60-page outline, and so on, until you ultimately have a 25-page outline of the class. This 25-page outline contains *all* the details you need for the final exam. You'll know it cold by the time this process is done. It will be the outline you study from and your first point of reference if the exam is open-book.[7]

Although the 25-page outline contains all the details, your work isn't done. To get the A, you need to see the big picture, which comes from making a one-page summary of the class. To get there, you cut down the 25-page outline to a 15-page outline, then a 10-page outline, and so on, until you have a 1-page overview. During this process, you focus on the major themes of the class and how those themes connect. In practice, this means focusing on every heading in your outline, knowing the cases and legal principles that fall under that heading, and understanding its relationship to every other heading. As discussed above, these headings should correspond to those on your syllabus or the casebook's table of contents.

1. The Value of a One-Page Outline

Your one-page final outline *is* the big picture of the class. By the time it's done, you will have memorized every major heading of your outline and understood the relationship between the headings. I have *never* seen the big picture *before* making a one-page outline, and I have *always* seen the big picture *after* making a one-page outline.

a. The Big Picture is More Important Than the Details

By the time 1L year ended, one of my advisees had the advice in this book down cold. As a first semester 3L, he had multiple job offers and the stress of law school was far behind him. He felt like

---

7. You prepare the exact same way for an open- or closed-book exam. By the time you're prepared for an open-book exam, you will almost never look at your outline anyway.

a carefree undergrad. The problem was that he hadn't been doing nearly enough school work.

About three weeks before his Evidence exam, he realized that it was time to learn some evidence. He hadn't read a single rule all semester, but he also hadn't missed a single class. Based on almost nothing but his meticulous class notes, he spent three weeks outlining the class and trying to learn all the details. On the night before the exam, he turned his 25-page outline of the rules, which he didn't know very well, into a 1-page summary of the entire class. The big picture clicked.

Although he barely knew the details, he got a *B*+, his worst grade since 1L year. Law school isn't like undergrad. Many students would be thrilled with a *B*+ after studying hard all semester. As one book puts it, in law school "B is the new A." I don't agree with that mentality *at all*, but it reflects how many law students think about grades. If they simply used the correct process, their time would lead to consistent *A*s.

The point of this story is that making a one-page outline is effective even if you don't know the details of a class as well as you should. Without knowing the details, you can do well enough on an exam by spotting the issues, stating what part of the class applies, and taking educated guesses at resolving the issues — all of which is possible if you see the big picture. To really seal the deal and bring the *B*+ to an *A*, you need to know the details of the class well enough to properly analyze the issues. That should always be your goal, even when you're a careless 3L.[8]

2. The Importance of Headings

As noted above, a crucial part of seeing the big picture is basing your outline on the syllabus. Before taking a single note on your reading, you should put the heading from the syllabus into your

---

8. You will be tempted to slack off once you have a job offer, but keep in mind that your first job will likely not be your last, and potential employers will look at your GPA for many years after law school.

notes. If you don't like the syllabus for some reason, use the headings from the casebook's table of contents instead.

Either way, make sure to organize your outline by areas of law, not by cases. The headings correspond to areas or law and thus give you perspective about where a particular homework assignment fits into the big picture of the class. This knowledge becomes crucial when you prepare for exams.[9]

3. Back Up Your Work Every Day

Every 3L knows a classmate who lost their outlines because of a computer problem. As a law student, you'll live on your computer and push the device to its limits. At some point, your computer might crash. This creates a $400 annoyance if your work is backed up, but it can sabotage an entire semester if your work is only saved locally. So make sure to constantly back up your notes. There are elegant, cloud-based ways to do this. You can also just attach your outlines to an e-mail and send them to yourself at the end of each day. If your work is backed up, then a *computer problem* won't cause an *academic problem*.

C. THE TIME CRUNCH

The time crunch is one of the biggest challenges of law school. You'll never feel like you have enough time to learn all the details of a class. The number of times you go through your outline depends much more on your final exam schedule than how comfortable you feel with the material.

When you finish going through your book notes and class notes just once, which usually happens on the last day of class, you'll have a roughly 100-page outline. From that point, it will take you five stressful and uninterrupted days of studying to completely prepare for the exam.

---

9. It also makes briefing cases easier. The legal issue in each case always relates to the heading on the syllabus.

But what if you don't have five days? Then you go through your outline fewer times and cut more content at once to reach 25 pages. Also, as my story about the Evidence exam makes clear, regardless of how well you know the details of a class, make sure to complete a one-page outline before the exam. Knowing how all the pieces connect is even more important than knowing the details.

The reason for this applies as much to law school as it does to the bar exam: Your grade is not just based on your knowledge of the law, but also on your ability to spot legal issues and identify which section of class applies. To go back to the college campus analogy, you earn points for realizing that your professor is asking for a thermometer and sending your professor to health services to find one. Even if you don't know where specifically the thermometer is located, you can still earn points for getting the professor to the right building. That's what seeing the big picture is all about.

Key Points

- To see the big picture, you need to understand the legal principle of each case, how that case fits into its section of class, and how each section of class connects. To achieve this, you'll outline all semester, starting from day one.
- Before class, brief the cases assigned for homework in as few sentences as possible. During class, pay close attention and write down everything your professor says. After class, while the material is fresh, spend 45 minutes shortening your class notes and synthesizing them with your book notes.
- By the last day of classes, you'll have 100 pages of notes for each class. Start cutting unnecessary details to turn those notes into 75 pages, then 60 pages, and so on, until you have a 25-page outline of the material. This is what you bring with you on an open book exam.
- You then go through that same process to turn your 25-page outline into a 1-page overview of the class. Once that's done, you'll see the big picture.

CHAPTER FIVE

COMMERCIAL OUTLINES DON'T WORK

(FOR THE MOST PART)

During my law school orientation, a number of speakers addressed my incoming class. One of the first, the president of the Student Government Association ("SGA"), told us about all the drinking and partying we had to look forward to over the next three years. We didn't have to worry, he assured us, because SGA sold used commercial outlines and hornbooks in their office. I didn't know what these were, but I was glad SGA sold them—they sounded helpful!

The next speaker was a professor who had been teaching at the law school for over 40 years. "Many of you will be lucky enough *not* to have Professor Ryckman," were the dean's exact words of introduction as she poked fun at her old friend. Professor Ryckman made his way to the podium and began, in his raspy, weathered voice: "Commercial outlines don't work, so don't use 'em! Trust the system. It's been around for a long time and it works!"

Once all was said and done, I still didn't know what commercial outlines were, but I was convinced they were the key to law school success. Little did I know that Professor Ryckman was right all along.

While they *might* allow students to scrape by, commercial outlines often cause more harm than good. The top students at your law school certainly don't rely on them. You might occasionally reference one for a very specific purpose, as explained below, but they're a non-essential tool at best.

A. WHAT ARE COMMERCIAL OUTLINES?

Commercial outlines are like the *Cliff's Notes* of law school. The term describes three different types of materials, only one of which is actually called a commercial outline:

(1) *Commercial Outline:* A book consisting of bullet points outlining uncontroversial and generally accepted statements about an area of law ("black letter law").

(2) *Canned Briefs:* Books containing summaries of the most notable cases in an area of law. These are often sold as unofficial supplements to specific casebooks, in which case they only summarize the cases found in those casebooks.

(3) *Hornbooks:* Some of these are scholarly treatises for advanced study of a branch of law. Others are much simpler books intended to help law students understand foundational concepts. Unlike bulleted commercial outlines, hornbooks read like traditional books.

B. WHY COMMERCIAL OUTLINES DON'T WORK

After you've spent hours and hours combing through your notes and wrestling with the material, you'll end up with a final product which resembles a commercial outline. It's tempting to just skip the annoying process and buy an outline. *After all,* the rationale goes, *what's the point of making your own outlines if someone else has already done the hard work for you?* Don't buy this reasoning.

The process of making an outline *is* the process of preparing for exams. The outline itself is the tangible result of your studying. By the time it's done, you'll know the material cold and every sentence will be packed with meaning. In contrast, studying from a commercial outline would be like reading the two goals of law school explained in Chapter Two without reading the rest of this book.[10] Put another way, making your own outlines is kind of like watching a superhero movie: You know it's going to end with the hero saving the world, but the value of the experience is everything leading up to that conclusion.

While commercial outlines might contain the information you *should have* extracted from the cases, they won't help you develop the analytical tools to extract the information yourself. Ironically, the fundamental problem with commercial outlines is also their biggest selling point: They give clear answers.

As you'll soon discover, there are no clear answers in cases or on law school exams. Courts make decisions based on an elaborate reasoning process which you're expected to replicate on final exams. Reading and briefing cases is the only way to learn this style of reasoning. Indeed, you should think of each case as a mini exam question, with the answer provided by the judge. On the actual exam, you'll play the judge's role.

Also, even the most objective professors stress certain aspects of a course and leave others out. Since commercial outlines aren't written by *your* professors, they often stress the "wrong" points. You'll hear stories about students who studied for a class using a commercial outline and then discussed issues on the final exam that the professor never covered during class.

As one professor explained: "The use of foreign material from a commercial outline or supplement usually leads to trouble. I recognize the foreign material quickly. If a student feels the need to use the supplement on the exam, odds are, I wasn't testing for the concept that they thought. The exam-taker probably had access to a more on-point and basic rule from the course that he could have applied. If the commercial outline gets it right, and you get it right,

---

10. As a reminder, those goals are to turn your 600 pages of reading and many hours of class time into a 25-page outline, and turn the 25-page outline into a 1-page overview of the class.

I will be forgiving. But the use of the supplement alone rings the 'they didn't understand the problem' bell."[11]

So is there any value to using commercial outlines? The answer isn't a hard no, but the value is definitely limited. Let's say you just finished briefing a complicated case and want to confirm your work before class. You might decide to spend literally five minutes checking a canned brief to ensure your own brief is in the right ballpark. It's an unnecessary step, since your professor will explain the case during class the next day, but that's an acceptable use of a commercial outline. Just note that you wouldn't do the same *after class*, at which point you'll have your professor's assessment of the material. That's what should end up in your outline.

Many students run into problems because they skip the import-ant part — reading the case and writing their own brief — and turn straight to a commercial outline for a quick answer. They might get by that way, but it's not a winning strategy.

Key Points

- The process of making an outline is the process of pre-paring for exams. The outline itself is the tangible result of your studying. By the time it's done, every sentence is packed with meaning.

- Commercial outlines might contain the information you should have extracted from the cases, but the entire point of making your own outlines is to learn the material and develop the analytical tools to extract that information yourself. Those are the very same tools you need to write strong exam answers.

- Commercial outlines often stress the "wrong" points because each professor has a unique approach to their area of law. Professors can usually tell when you rely on foreign materials instead of your book notes and class notes.

---

11. Anonymous Law Professor, *All You Ever Wanted To Know About Law School Exams*, Nov. 30, 1999, https://abovethelaw.com/2009/11/all-you-ever-wanted-to-know-about-law-school-exams/.

CHAPTER SIX

TRUSTING YOUR INTUITION AND TALKING TO PROFESSORS

During my third year of law school, I took a class called Securities Regulation. For one particularly bothersome issue, I couldn't understand the statute, the book was unclear, and my class notes were silent. I e-mailed my professor for guidance, and he responded with a clear explanation. To my surprise, the issue was one of three questions on the final exam, and in turn, responsible for one-third of my grade.

While most top students agree that talking to professors is useful, many believe the value is more subtle than what I just described. They assure me it was a "fluke" and "it could only happen like that once." I concede that speaking with professors doesn't usually result in having an exam answer in your notes. But it happened to me *twice*, in two different classes.

To maximize your chances of stumbling on an exam question, be very careful not to reject your own thoughts while studying. Many of us have the tendency to stumble on a complicated issue or a subtle inconsistency and continue on with our studying as if we never saw it. However, these subtleties are exactly the kinds of issues professors like to explore on final exams. If you think of an obscure issue while studying but don't ask your professor about it, you might end up having to provide your own explanation at the end of the semester.

This is not to imply that you should only e-mail professors about subtleties. Often enough, 90% of the class is confused about a glaring problem but very few students, if any, ask the professor to clarify. You'll have unique insight into the final exam if you're among the students who ask.

Moreover, at many law schools, professors can raise students' grades for participation, which isn't limited to speaking in class. Indeed, don't make too many comments in class, lest your classmates label you a "classhole." Most of your communication with professors should take place out of class, rather than in front of a 100-person audience. Professors also raise grades for the few students who regularly e-mail questions and go to office hours.

Staying in touch with professors has indirect benefits too. They know lots of successful lawyers and are often willing to reach out on behalf of students. One of my classmates got a job at Sullivan and Cromwell because a professor made a casual call on his behalf.

You also might need a recommendation at some point down the line. Who's going to write a more persuasive letter, a professor who knows you personally or a professor who vaguely remembers you from class?

Key Points

- E-mail professors questions and visit professors during office hours to discuss the material. They'll be glad to answer your questions.
- Engaging with professors has three benefits:
  - You'll gain valuable insight into the material for the final exam.
  - At many law schools, professors can raise your grade for good participation.
  - Your professors will get to know you and be in a better position to write references.

CHAPTER SEVEN

HOW TO ACE EXAMS

Once you see the big picture, you'll do well on the final exam. A few points regarding exams are nevertheless worth mentioning.

A. THE RISK OF TYPING EVERYTHING YOU KNOW

In almost every class, your entire grade depends on one final exam. The 30-or-so minutes before that exam epitomize the cliché of cutting the tension in the room with a knife.

Here's a snapshot of exam day: You haven't gone out in weeks because you've spent every free minute studying. You finally managed to see the big picture the night before the exam, but you were so nervous that you didn't get much sleep. You wake up and drag yourself to the testing room full of adrenaline but with that tired feeling in your eyes. You sit down and quickly realize that your palms are sweating and your heart is racing. It feels like your entire legal career is on the line. You try to go over that outline again, but it's of no use ("If I don't know it by now...") so you go pee. At least *that's* still within your control.

Your classmates are equally nervous, but unlike you, some of them feel the need to ask other classmates questions about last-minute issues they anxiously thought up that morning. While these issues are exceedingly unlikely to come up on the exam, hearing about them makes you even more nervous because you hadn't thought of them yourself. Just as your fear reaches a crescendo, the proctor utters those three fateful words, "you may begin."

You break the exam's seal to discover a bizarre fact pattern taking place in a 51st State called MassaTexYork. The two-page story begins with roommates named Dill and Pickles. (You're sure the professor meant to be funny, but you're in no mood for jokes.) It turns out Dill got drunk and stole an airplane. He was flying to California to kill his archnemesis, Relish, but instead, accidentally killed his roommate, Pickles, who somehow fell asleep in the wheel-well of the plane. There was also a police chase, a few injuries, and maybe even a train wreck.

You struggle through these facts praying that your professor put a question at the end to serve as a beacon. To your chagrin, the "question" consists of a single word: "Discuss."

You start to kind-of FREAK OUT. You look up to see how your classmates are doing and it appears that John, who you never thought was very smart anyway, is already typing.

You will be nervous and you will have a ton of law floating around your head. If you're not careful, John's typing might be just enough to scare you into incoherently spewing *everything* you know about the area of law onto your computer screen. As long as you walk into the exam with a clear strategy (and earplugs!) this temptation will not lead you astray.

B. THE STRATEGY

If you approach a final exam thinking you must resolve the entire hypothetical or give one answer to the entire question, your task will seem impossible. Rather, you should break down the question into small, manageable parts and address each part individually. This is called "issue spotting." Almost every law school exam question, no matter how complicated it might seem, consists of a number of issues that you've covered throughout the semester. To do well, you need to address those issues one by one, mechanically and methodically.

Because each issue is only worth a few points, you should address as many issues as possible, even if it means discussing them in less detail than you'd like. If you spend an entire exam addressing the two issues you know especially well, you simply can't earn a high grade, regardless of the quality of your analysis.

C. "IRAC"

Most professors expect you to use the "IRAC" method to write exams. IRAC stands for:

- Issue
- Rule
- Application
- Conclusion

For each issue you spot on the exam, you begin by stating the **issue** and explaining the relevant **rule** of law — *i.e.*, how the same issue was resolved in some decision you read earlier in the semester. You then **apply** the rule to the facts of the exam and draw a **conclusion** about how a court would resolve the issue.

Assume you're taking a torts exam and part of the two-page fact pattern reads as follows:

> A young pilot named Maverick has been prone to fits of sneezing his whole life. These usually come unexpectedly and involve Maverick 'achu-ing' at least ten times in seriatim. During one especially severe episode, Maverick briefly lost control of his plane and flew so close to the radio tower that its operator, frazzled by the fly-by, sustained injuries by spilling a mug of hot coffee all over himself.... The case was heard by Judge Iceman in the fictional State of Old York."[12]

---

12. Professors frequently make exams more amusing (at least to themselves) by basing questions on obscure characters from the pop culture of their youth. This

This paragraph would be one of many issues on the exam. After spotting this issue, you would address it as follows:

> *[Start by stating the issue.]* One issue is whether Maverick ("respondent") would be liable for the tower operator's ("movant's") injuries. *[Go on to state the rule.]* The rule from Hammontree[13] is that a party is only liable for another's injuries if the party acted negligently. *[Then analyze how the rule applies to your facts.]* The movant would argue that it is negligent for a person prone to sneezing fits to fly an airplane. The respondent would argue that it is not negligent because any pilot might be distracted by a sneeze. The movant would respond that most pilots are not subject to the same kind of severe sneezing as the respondent, and unlike the defendant in Hammontree, the respondent did not take any steps to prevent sneezing fits while flying, thereby making otherwise reasonable behavior negligent. *[End by stating your conclusion.]* I believe Judge Iceman would conclude that the respondent was "dangerous" and rule in favor of the movant. Unlike most people, the respondent was subject to especially severe sneezing fits which made it unsafe for him to fly. Under Hammontree, the respondent should have taken some steps to make his sneezing fits less likely. By not doing so, he was negligent.

Note that I refer to the relevant actors as *movant* and *respondent*, rather than *plaintiff, defendant, appellant,* or *appellee.* The terms movant and respondent apply regardless of whether the parties are at trial, appealing a trial court decision, or appealing an appellate court decision. You can call any party a movant, as long as the party is asking the court to do something, and you can

---

particular question is based on the cinematic masterpiece Top Gun.

13. Most professors would also be fine with you calling this the "seizure car accident case" or something similar. You generally do not need to remember case names on exams, although it does sound better if you do.

call any party a respondent, as the long as the party is responding to the movant.

Here is why this avoids a lot of unnecessary confusion: The terms plaintiff and defendant only apply at the trial level. On appeal, the parties go by appellant and appellee. But if the appellee appeals the appellate decision, then the appellee becomes the appellant and vice versa. As long as you use *movant* and *respondent*, you won't need to worry about any of that confusion.

For the *application* prong of this answer, I used a back-and-forth exchange between the parties. While this is often an effective method, some questions don't lend themselves to an exchange, in which case it's fine to answer in your own voice.

What if you recognize some obscure reference on the exam? Is it appropriate to make a joke about it? Nothing can replace your knowledge of the professor's personality based on a semester of class. Even if your professor is of the light-hearted variety, you should never make a joke unless you're absolutely confident that your analysis is spot on. Otherwise, it might seem like you don't take the class or exam seriously. If your analysis *is* spot-on, a joke tells your professor, "I'm just that good." Obviously, that's the goal, but when in doubt, don't make jokes.

Finally, note that the sample answer above only addresses one issue. On an exam you would address every issue the same way. The more issues you identify and analyze, the more points you earn.

D. OUTLINING AND HIGHLIGHTING

Some people find it helpful to briefly outline their exam answers on paper before typing them out. I didn't outline every answer, but I was more likely to do so if the fact pattern was long or especially complicated. Even if outlining means you're writing while other people are typing, it's not a big deal—the ten minutes you spend outlining will make typing the answer much faster.

You don't have to outline your answer, but at the very least, make sure to highlight each excerpt of the exam question which gives rise to an issue. That way, you'll know what issues you shouldn't miss when answering the question.

E. TIME MANAGEMENT

Poor time management is the most common reason that well-prepared students underperform on exams. You'll hear stories about students who never answered an entire question because they ran out of time. Indeed, the classmate I wrote about in the introduction was brought to tears by this very mistake.

Before exams, most professors will tell you how much time to spend on each question. If a professor does not volunteer a suggestion, be sure to ask. If the professor refuses to answer, spend the first two minutes of your exam counting the number of questions and allocating your time accordingly. Needless to say, bring the same kind of watch you'd bring for the LSAT.

However you arrive at your time allocation, don't deviate from it, even if you find a new issue at the last minute. It's very tempting to spend an extra minute here and an extra few seconds there, but that's how students end up with nine minutes for a sixty minute final question. If you're out of time on a question but catch such an important issue that you simply can't move on without addressing it, then quickly explain the issue in your answer and leave a note to the following effect: "Unfortunately, I am out of time and cannot fully analyze this issue." You might have time to go back at the end of the exam. If not, your professor might give you a couple points just for spotting the issue.

1. A Wrinkle Regarding the First Question

I always allocated an extra few minutes to the first question of each final exam: first, because it would take me a little while to stop being nervous and actually start thinking, and second, because first impressions are very important. If your professor reads a solid first answer, you're more likely to have the benefit of the doubt for the remaining answers.[14]

F. PRACTICE MAKES PERFECT, OR DOES IT?

Your school will have old exams on file for each class. Some students use these to take practice exams while studying. Here's the challenge: You'll never feel like you have enough time in law school. Spending three hours on a practice exam means losing three hours of outlining. Moreover, attempting a practice exam before you've mastered the material can just make you more nervous.

You need to know your outline cold and see the big picture before being able to confidently spot and analyze the issues on an exam. If you try doing that before seeing the big picture, you might psych yourself out over an exam that actually isn't that hard.

So here's my advice: If you finish your 25-page outline and 1-page overview, know the material cold, and still have a couple days before the exam, then go ahead and take a practice exam. The reality is that, more often than not, you'll find yourself making the one-page overview on the day before the exam. That means you won't have time to take a practice exam, which is totally fine. Even if you do finish the whole process a couple days early for a particular class, your time might be better spent preparing for the next class' exam rather than taking a practice test. Of course, if you have the time, then it certainly can't hurt.

Key Points

- Typical exam questions consist of a number of issues that you've covered throughout the semester. To tackle long and complicated questions, you should break them down into small, manageable parts and address each part individually. This is called "issue spotting."

---

14. This assumes that your professor reads through your entire exam, rather than grading everyone's first question first, second question second, and so on.

- Analyze the issues using the IRAC method: identify the issue; state the rule of law; apply the rule to the facts; and draw a conclusion.
- Each issue is only worth a few points, so you should address as many issues as possible rather than overanalyzing the ones you know especially well.
- Before you start writing, either make a brief outline of your answer or, at the very least, highlight each excerpt of the exam question that gives rise to an issue.
- Ask professors how much time to spend on each exam question. If they don't tell you, then start the exam by counting the questions and allocating your time. Don't go over time on a particular question or you will run out of time on the others.
- Refer to the relevant actors as movant and respondent to avoid confusion.
- Bring ear plugs and the same kind of watch you'd take to the LSAT.
- Don't worry too much about practice exams. Your time is much better spent outlining and mastering the material.

CHAPTER EIGHT

THE IMPORTANCE OF 2L AND 3L CLASS SELECTION

When I think of selecting classes for 2L and 3L year, the story of the Three Little Pigs comes to mind. Most students barely think about class selection, spend a few minutes signing up for whatever classes they can get into, and end up building a house out of straw. When the Big Bad Wolf comes along in the form of final exams, he easily blows the house down.

I'll give you an example: After working for a few years after college, one of my classmates came to law school with a very serious attitude. He recognized law school would be difficult but was willing to work extremely hard to make the most of it. As planned, he studied a lot first year, stayed off the social radar, and ended up with above-average grades. When it came time for second- and third-year class selection, he loaded up on hard classes without considering his workload or final exam schedule. He once managed to have a final exam the day after classes ended and two other exams two days in a row. In the end, his grades fell below average, dragging down his first year GPA and making it difficult to find a job.

As my friend learned the hard way, your 2L and 3L class selections play a pivotal role in both your grades and quality of life as an upperclassman. Many students indiscriminately load up on hard classes like Corporate Finance, Securities Regulation, Bankruptcy, and Tax. They don't even know what these subjects are but take them anyway, *in the same semester,* falsely believing that's what good students are supposed to do. They don't pause to consider time management, stress level, or their final exam schedule, and ultimately, their grades suffer.

To build a house out of brick, you should spend hours thoughtfully setting up your second- and third-year schedules. Before I explain how to create a good schedule, let's briefly discuss the difference between seminars and curved courses.

A. SEMINARS VERSUS CURVED COURSES

At most law schools, 1Ls only take curved classes.[15] In contrast, second and third year students have the option of taking small, college-style classes which aren't subject to a curve. These are called seminars.

Seminars tend to be easier than the 100-person curved classes you'll take as a 1L. Grades are usually based on papers rather than finals, and professors are more likely to give out As. Since grades are more subjective, personal relationships with professors become especially important.

In contrast, upperclass curved courses are often more rigorous than 1L curved courses. The reading assignments are longer and the subject matter is often more complicated. While a number of curved courses are somewhat necessary for the bar exam, you should carefully pick the right subjects and spread them out evenly over your four upperclass semesters.

As a general rule, your 2L and 3L schedules should include one or two curved courses per semester, and the remainder of your classes should be seminars.

B. SOME COMMON CONCERNS

Students generally have three concerns when registering for classes: (1) being prepared for the bar exam; (2) being prepared for

---

15. This means professors must give an even distribution of high, average, and low grades.

legal practice; and (3) having a transcript which appeals to employers. Surprisingly, many students don't consider the equally important issue of how their class selections will impact their grades. By thinking carefully about your schedule, you can address all of these concerns. Let's discuss them one-by-one.

1. The Bar Exam

The "bar exam" really consists of two exams: (1) the Multi-State Bar Exam, which is the same for everyone; and (2) a state-specific exam, which tests how individual states approach the same few areas of law.

Like most law students, you'll likely take a bar preparation course the summer after graduating. This course covers everything you need to know for the bar exam. While you can easily learn each subject if you haven't taken the underlying class in law school, the material is easier to learn if you've already studied it once.

Luckily, the bar only covers a few subjects and you will take most of them during 1L year, when you have no control over your schedule. As a 2L and 3L, you should structure your schedule so that the one or two curved courses you take each semester are subjects which appear on the bar.

The most important bar exam subjects are the ones tested on the Multistate Bar Exam. These are Contracts, Constitutional Law, Criminal Law, Criminal Procedure, Civil Procedure, Evidence, Real Estate, and Torts.[16] Note that many popular law school classes, such as Tax and Bankruptcy, aren't tested.

Even if you take only one bar-related class per upperclass semester, you will take almost every major subject by the time you graduate. To the extent you don't take one or two of the subjects in law school, you'll learn them in your bar preparation course over the summer.

---

16. You can check an individual state's bar websites to determine what subjects the state exam covers. Also, BarBri puts out a helpful state-by-state list of bar exam subjects.

2. Law Practice

With a few exceptions, you'll learn everything you need to practice law once you start practicing. If you're starting in a department which does general commercial litigation or general corporate work, you'll do just fine even if you haven't taken many specialized classes. If you know you'll be working in a highly specialized practice area, such as bankruptcy or securities, then you might want to take a couple curved courses relating to your practice area. You should only take those classes once you have an offer in hand, and you should make sure the rest of your classes are seminars.

3. How Your Schedule Appears to Employers

Some students are justifiably concerned about how their class selections appear to potential employers. As long as your seminars are substantive classes about real areas of law, you will have nothing to worry about during interviews. For example, Insurance Law and Accounting Law are sometimes taught as seminars. An employer won't think twice if they see either class on your transcript. In contrast, seminars like Philosophy of Law and Tort Theory sound fluffy and irrelevant to practice. As long as your seminars are more like the former, your transcript will look good to employers.

Also, keep in mind that the hardest part of interviewing is getting your foot in the door. Employers decide whether to talk to you based on a resume with your GPA on it. Regardless of the classes used to arrive at the GPA, a student with high grades is almost always more appealing to employers than a student with low grades.

C. THE VALUE OF PEER EVALUATION

Whether you're signing up for a seminar or curved course, ask your school's registrar for student reviews of the professor. If your law school doesn't maintain reviews, then check websites like www. ratemyprofessor.com. In any event, you should only take classes with professors who receive high reviews. Be sure to read reviews of the *professor* rather than reviews of the *class*. If Professor Schmidt has never taught Constitutional Law, check out her reviews from Criminal Law.

Also, to the extent your school provides data about grade distributions from old classes, be sure to take professors who grade leniently. Taking a seminar with a professor who usually gives half the class a low grade defeats the purpose of taking a seminar.

D. EXAM SCHEDULES

You should have access to the coming semester's exam schedule during the class registration process. As I mentioned above, from the moment you finish going through your book notes and class notes just once, you will need five stressful and uninterrupted days of studying to see the big picture and feel completely ready for the exam. The more time you have, the better prepared you'll be.

When you set up your schedule, make sure to space your exams as far apart as possible. Never sign up for a class if the exam is scheduled a day after classes end. Since you have the option, choose classes which will give you as much time as possible to study. Likewise, never choose classes which have exams scheduled too close to each other. If you take two curved courses in one semester, make sure the exams are at least a week apart. The more time you have to prepare, the more times you can go through your outline and the better you'll perform.

E. CONCLUSION

Finalizing your class schedule should take many hours and a great deal of thought. Between contemplating which courses to take, which professors to take them with, and what your final exam schedule will look like, picking classes should be an involved, time-consuming process. If you pick the right classes, your stress level will be relatively low, your exam schedule will give you ample time to prepare, and your hard work will yield *A*s.

Key Points

- Your 2L and 3L class selections play a pivotal role in both your grades and quality of life as an upperclassman.
- At many law schools, 2Ls and 3Ls can take seminars that aren't subject to a curve. If you have this option, you should register for one or two curved courses per semester and balance out your schedule with seminars.
- To make studying for the bar easier, the curved classes you take as a 2L and 3L should be classes that are tested on the bar.
- To ensure that your transcript appeals to employers, pick seminars that cover substantive areas of law (think Insurance Law rather than Philosophy of Law).
- If you're planning to practice in a highly-specialized area, then it's a good idea to take some curved courses related to that area (just not at the expense of your GPA).
- Read reviews of professors before registering for classes. Likewise, if your law school makes grade distributions available, sign up for classes with professors whose distributions are reasonable.
- Carefully review the exam date for each class. Register for classes that give you as much time as possible to prepare for each exam and leave multiple days between exams.

CHAPTER NINE

TAKING CARE OF YOURSELF

CULTIVATING HEALTH, HAPPINESS, AND A RESILIENT MINDSET

A. THE WRONG WAY

During 1L year, I had a friend who claimed he didn't have time for anything but schoolwork. He stayed up late into the night reading casebooks and then consumed energy drinks throughout the day to stay awake. He saw food and exercise as mere distractions from studying, so he stopped going to the gym and usually ate unhealthy fast food because it was the quickest option.

While he spent most of his time on schoolwork, he took occasional breaks to go out drinking with classmates. Ironically, this method of "relaxation" had the opposite effect: Once every week or two, he would wake up hungover and foggy, finding it even harder to understand the complicated material which made him stressed in the first place.

Many of your classmates will be completely sedentary, subsist on caffeine and fast food, and turn to alcohol to relax. As you might imagine, students who live this way look and feel very different as graduating 3Ls than they did as incoming 1Ls. Obviously, their grades also suffer.

B. A BETTER ALTERNATIVE

Countless studies show that exercise and good nutrition reduce stress, increase happiness, and sharpen concentration. Likewise, sleeping seven to eight hours per night, rather than staying up and squeezing in an extra hour or two of work, is shown to make students *more* productive even though they spend slightly *less* time studying.

The first year of law school is a seemingly endless cycle of reading and outlining. You'll never feel like you have enough time to get everything done, which makes it especially easy to neglect your health. Don't fall into that trap: Treat exercise, good nutrition, and rest as essential and non-negotiable elements of your academic success.

To be clear, I'm not suggesting that you completely abstain from alcohol and spend every free minute running and eating sprouted tofu. You'll have fun and make friends in law school. It's totally reasonable to go out for drinks and enjoy nice dinners. Just make sure to keep things balanced.

C. SLEEP BEFORE EXAMS

Sleeping enough is especially important before exams. You'll be sharper and exams will feel easier if you walk in after a solid eight hours of sleep. As a 1L, you'll have a consistent schedule that's set by the school. On most days, you should expect classes to start around 9:00 am.

If you're one of those people who goes to sleep at 9:00 pm and wakes up at 5:00 am, then god bless you; you're in great shape. For the night owls among you, try to go to sleep no later than midnight. That way you can wake up at 8:00 am, grab a quick breakfast, and head off to class. Here's where the night owls can run into trouble: After classes end, you'll have a week or so to focus entirely on preparing for exams (this is often called "reading week" or "reading period"). Much like 1L classes, most exams take place around 9:00 am. If your reading week involves studying late into the night and waking up around noon, your internal clock will shift and you won't be able to fall asleep at a reasonable time before your exams. The simple solution is to stick with the midnight-to-8:00 am sleep schedule through reading week. Then you'll be rested and right on schedule once exams start.

Let's say, despite your best efforts, you have a terrible night before an exam. Perhaps you were nervous, your sleep schedule was off, or for whatever reason, you wake up genuinely feeling terrible. If that happens, then go to the law school's health center, explain you don't feel well, and ask for a note documenting the visit. That will allow you to take a self-administered final exam at a later time. Of course, use great discretion when choosing this option and don't do it more than once.

D. A RESILIENT, GROWTH MINDSET

I'm personally fascinated by the field of positive psychology, which offers tremendous insights into how happiness contributes to all areas of human performance. For a great overview, I recommend a book called *The Happiness Advantage* by Shawn Achor. For now, with brevity in mind, let me give you some key takeaways which are especially relevant to law students.

Even with a good strategy, law school won't be easy. You'll have hard days, difficult classes, and unexpected challenges. Whatever happens, try to maintain a resilient, growth mindset. Keep setbacks in perspective and use them as learning experiences to achieve future success. As one article explains:

For students in a fixed mindset, law school is a place that has two types of students: the smart ones who will go off and do some amazing things at the most prestigious firms, and the not-so-smart ones who will get the bottom of the barrel jobs doing mediocre things. For students in a fixed mindset, they are likely to view setbacks, such as lower-than-expected grades, as a sign that they are incapable.

On the other hand, students in a growth mindset who understand that abilities can be developed, tend to look at the inevitable setbacks differently. They view law school as a place that can provide them with opportunities to grow and learn. They actively seek feedback and strategies to tweak their approaches so that they achieve greater improvement and outcomes the next time around.[17]

As I hope this book makes clear, you can learn the right skills to succeed in law school. So when that mid-term grade isn't what you expected, your legal writing assignment didn't go as planned, or the reading was surprisingly challenging, ask yourself: What will I do differently next time to avoid the same outcome? How will I change my strategy to continuously improve?

Of course, the issue might be larger than a bad grade on a single exam. Did you pick up this book during winter break after a tough first semester, or in the summer after a tough first year? That's great. As you've realized, the best time to learn these strategies is before law school starts. Luckily for you, the second-best time is *right now*. Bravo for trying to understand what went wrong and how to fix it. That's the essence of a growth mindset. You'll have a blank slate next semester to implement a new strategy and hit the ground running. And if you stay at the very top of your second- and third-year classes, you'll still graduate with honors and reap all the benefits that entails.

Key Points

- Countless studies show that exercise and good nutrition reduce stress, increase happiness, and sharpen concentration.
- Studies also show that sleeping seven to eight hours per night, rather than staying up and squeezing in an extra hour of work, makes students more productive even though they spend less time studying.
- Night owls should be careful not to throw off their sleep schedule during reading week. If you spend the week going to sleep late into the night and waking up at noon,

17. Eduardo Briceno and Dawn Young, *A Growth Mindset for Law School Success*, Sep. 12, 2017, abaforlawstudents.com/2017/09/12/growth-mindset-law-school-success/.

it will be impossible to fall asleep at a reasonable hour and wake up rested for a 9:00 am exam.

- If you have a terrible night before an exam and genuinely feel sick in the morning, then go to your school health center, get a note documenting the visit, and postpone your exam. Treat this as a one-time option.
- Do your best to keep setbacks in perspective and maintain a growth mindset, always thinking about how to improve in the future.

CHAPTER TEN

EMPLOYMENT

THE LIGHT AT THE END OF THE TUNNEL

As a first semester 1L, don't worry about finding a job. Just focus on excelling in your classes by implementing the strategies described above. For now, you can read this chapter as a sneak-preview of the job search and then come back to it during winter break.

Obviously, this entire book is about doing well in law school. It's certainly an important goal, but let's take the long view for a moment. When you start law school, you'll be scared from all directions into thinking your 1L grades and alma mater will make or break your legal career. Here's a little exercise for you. Go on the websites of some of the top firms in the country: Cravath, Kirkland & Ellis, Davis Polk, etc. Click on the "attorneys" tab and search by law school. You'll find numerous attorneys who went to low-ranking schools and countless others who graduated without academic honors or distinctions.

I'll tell you a little story from my own experience. I started practicing law in the middle of the Great Recession. On my first day of work, my firm's biggest client, Lehman Brothers, collapsed. As you might imagine, firms were laying off lawyers left and right. At my firm, the structured finance practice was hit hardest. Three of their five first-year associates were laid off. Two of them had gone to top ten law schools, while three had gone to somewhat less prestigious schools. Once all was said and done, the two associates from the top schools were gone, while two of the other lawyers still had jobs.

How did it work out that way? Since the department had been slow for a long time, none of the associates had much work. The associates who were laid off sat at their desks reading the *New York Times*. The associates who kept their jobs were hustling—walking around the office meeting partners, socializing with senior associates, asking for pro bono work, and volunteering to write articles. They did everything possible to put themselves out there, and it ended up saving their jobs.

Once you start practicing, you'll quickly see that you can't rest on past accomplishments. On the flip side, once your foot's in the door, you shouldn't feel constrained by past academic challenges. Your coworkers and supervisors will care about two things: *1. Do you produce good work that's delivered on time?* and *2. Are you pleasant and reliable?* If the answer to both questions is *yes*, then you will excel at work and nobody will care about your academic background. If the answer to either question is *no*, then you will struggle at work... and nobody will care about your academic background.

Of course, the first challenge is getting your foot in the door, and that's where your grades are most relevant. If you earn high grades, your job search will certainly be easier. If you wish your GPA was a bit better, don't worry; it's not an insurmountable obstacle. You'll just have to be more aggressive about finding a job.

A. THE MULTIPLE MEANINGS OF "FINDING A JOB"

Over the three years of law school, students undertake three different job searches: first, you will find a summer position after your first year, then you will find a summer position after your second year, and ultimately, you will find a full-time job after graduation.

The traditional wisdom of the job search is that first year students take whatever they can get (including unpaid internships), second year students seek paid summer associate positions at law firms, and third year students either have an offer from their summer associate position or go back on the job market to find a full-time position. Your strategy for all three job searches should be the same.

B. THE FOUNDATIONS OF FINDING A JOB

Your law school has a career office that exists for the sole purpose of helping you obtain gainful employment. The office is staffed by knowledgeable career counselors who can provide sample resumes and cover letters, conduct mock interviews, and assist in myriad other ways. As a first step, you should enlist their help with a couple foundational elements of the job search:

First, you need a well-written resume and cover letter. You should start by reading some samples that you obtain online or from your school's career office. Based on those samples, draft a resume and cover letter on your own, and then ask a career counselor (or better yet, more than one) for edits and feedback.

Second, read about the most common law firm interview questions, and participate in a few mock interviews. Career counselors conduct mock interviews on campus, and they also connect students with alumni, who conduct mock interviews at their law firms. That experience will make you much more comfortable with the interview process.

Once you're satisfied that you have a well-edited resume, thoughtful cover letter, and reasonable comfort level with interviews, you can begin the job-seeking strategies explained below.

C. THE STANDARD PATH

The career office will explain your school's on-campus interview process. As the name suggests, employers come to your school and interview students right on campus. This is how many students, especially those with the highest grades, find their jobs. But let's say on-campus interviews don't work out for you; perhaps your first-year grades weren't as good as they could have been or you got a little nervous during the interviews themselves. Don't get discouraged. You'll still find a good job if you engage in the disciplined process described below.

D. BEYOND ON-CAMPUS INTERVIEWS

Finding a job is a process of collecting rejections. If you are sufficiently aggressive in your job search, you will receive infinitely more negative than positive responses. That's a good thing. You need the "nos" to get to a "yes."

I still have an envelope of every law firm rejection letter that I've ever received. As a student, I collected those rejections with pride because they meant I was being active in the job search. In a very real way, each rejection brought me one step closer to a job offer. I would only get nervous if a week or two went by without any rejections. When that happened, it made me question whether I was applying to enough firms.

Keep in mind what many students do: They try their luck with on-campus interviews, apply to a few firms on the career office's website, and then fall into a state of misery and despair when the 30 or so employers they contacted reject them.

Let's assume you want a job at a law firm but the on-campus interview process doesn't work out.[18] Here's what you can expect: For every 100 firms you contact, most will simply ignore you, some will give you the courtesy of a rejection letter, and *one* or maybe *two* will offer you an interview.

That doesn't sound like much, but if you send out a few hundred inquiries and land four to five interviews, you will likely receive a job offer. Keep in mind, very few students go through the process I'm describing. Often enough, you'll be the only student contacting

---

18. If you don't plan to work at a law firm, that's totally fine. Just replace the word "firm" with "judge," "non-profit," "real estate investment trust," or any other employer. The same exact principle applies.

the firms in question. That means those three to four interviews are with firms that might only be speaking with *you*, which makes each interview far more likely to lead to a job than the on-campus interviews at your law school, in which each firm meets with dozens of applicants.

How will you find the time to submit a few hundred job inquiries while preparing for classes, outlining for exams, and doing everything else described in this book? It's fairly simple: send five to ten applications per day, every day, using a standard e-mail in which you only change the name of the recipient. If you want to get really fancy about it, buy some resume paper and, in addition to the e-mail, send each firm a hard copy of your cover letter and resume.[19] If you send an average of seven inquiries per day for two months, you'll have contacted roughly 400 firms, collected an impressive stack of rejection letters, and landed about four interviews.

E. FINDING POTENTIAL EMPLOYERS

To find all these firms, go on Martindale.com and NALPDirectory.com, and run a search for the firms within 20 miles of where you want to live. You can sort by litigation, corporate, or whatever practice area interests you.

Regarding *who* to contact at each firm, look for a partner who went to your college or law school. If you can't find one, just reach out to the managing partner. Your natural inclination might be to contact the hiring manager, but that person's job is to screen resumes and decide which ones are worthy of the partners' attention. You can bypass that process by contacting the partners directly. Very occasionally, a partner might respond and ask you to e-mail the hiring manager. In this case your e-mail will say, "I spoke to Ms. Smith, one of the litigation partners, who suggested

---

19. In case the snail mail approach seems dated, think of the last time you received a handwritten envelope from an individual. You opened it, right? Most of our mail consists of mass-produced advertisements, so handwritten letters easily rise above the noise.

I reach out to you," and suddenly your resume will make it to the top of the stack.

F. MAKE SURE TO HUSTLE

I have a friend who works at one of the most prestigious firms in the country but went to a law school you've probably never heard of. Perhaps you even stumbled on his profile while doing the search I recommended above! When I asked how he did it, he explained that he's always been a "doer" and he generally finds himself surrounded by passive observers.

In law school, he simply did more than his classmates. He formed relationships with professors, joined various lawyers' groups, and went out of his way to e-mail and meet with successful lawyers whenever possible. He would find a law firm partner who went to his college, read an article written by that partner, and then send the partner an e-mail about how interesting he found the article. In the process, he would *happen* to ask whether the firm had any openings for summer associates.

He met with every lawyer willing to talk to him, and ultimately applied to three times as many jobs as his classmates. Of the hundreds of lawyers he e-mailed and the dozens he met in person, he managed to impress at least one partner at a top firm, and it got him an amazing job.

Does this seem above and beyond what your classmates will do? That's exactly the point. You have to hustle. If you do more than seems reasonable to find a job, and you keep pressing forward in the face of rejection and adversity, then you will end up with a great job. And once you do, read that book I mentioned in the preface: *The Curmudgeon's Guide to Practicing Law* by Mark Herrmann. It'll make you a better associate.

Key Points

- Draft a strong resume and cover letter using samples that you find online and in your school's career office, and then ask a career counselor for feedback and edits.

- Research the most common law firm interview questions, draft your go-to answers, and ask your school's career office to help you set up mock interviews for practice.
- The easiest, most straightforward way to find a job is your school's on-campus interview program.
- If the on-campus interview program doesn't work out for you, then you should send your resume and cover letter to five to ten firms a day, every day, until you have a job offer.
- Finding a job is a process of collecting rejections. For every 100 employers you contact, 1 or 2 might invite you for an interview. The rejections are a sign that you're being sufficiently aggressive in your job search.
- To find potential employers, go on Martindale.com and NALPDirectory.com, and filter by geography and practice area.

CONCLUSION

I started this book by explaining my own fears during the first days of law school. I felt like everyone around me was a star in college but the curve meant only a few of us could stand out. That assessment was accurate, of course, but it was also based on a fundamentally flawed assumption.

Like most new law students, I thought that the hardest-working, smartest students earned the highest grades. But what happens when 300 top students with similar LSATs and GPAs try to outwork and outsmart each other? A few get lucky while the majority don't.

Hard work and intelligence aren't enough to succeed in law school. That's where *strategy* comes in. The few students who use the correct strategy rise to the top of the class. The majority of students struggle to stay afloat while relying on tools that worked in college but are inadequate for law school.

By reading this book and internalizing its lessons, you've already done more to prepare than the majority of your classmates. As a 1L, you'll compete in a different league: You and a few other students will fight for the very top grades, and the small group of you will vastly outperform everyone else.

Are you still feeling a bit nervous about the experience? There's a saying that nothing reduces anxiety better than action. So if that's how you're feeling, don't stop with this book. Read what others have to say on the subject. Take a law school preparation class (check out

LEEWS). Ask successful lawyers for their best advice. Speak to law students about what they wish they had known before law school started. You'll see the same themes over and over again, and in the process, you'll add valuable tools to your arsenal.

Even with the best strategy law school won't be easy—but nothing of value is easy. The most successful people constantly test themselves against new challenges. With every obstacle you over-come, you build tools and skills that will stick with you for life. One day, you'll nostalgically look back at this time and reflect on how much it's contributed to the person you've become.

I wish you the very best of luck.

PRACTICE BRIEFING
HAMMONTREE V. JENNER

As explained in Chapter Two, courts make many statements about the law. Each case appears in your casebook because of how the court resolved one legal issue. If you focus only on the statements of law concerning that issue, your briefs will stay short. To help identify that issue, check your syllabus and the book's table of contents. The legal issue will always relate to the subject noted in those materials. Before reading the case below, note the sample table of contents and syllabus entries.

> **Class Syllabus:** The following case might appear in a section called, "When is a Defendant Liable for an Unintended Accident?"
>
> **Casebook's Table of Contents:** The following case might appear in a section called, "When Courts Impose Strict Liability."

Hammontree v. Jenner, 20 Cal. App. 3d 528 (Cal. App. 1971)

Plaintiff Maxine Hammontree and her husband sued defendant for personal injuries and property damage arising out of an automobile accident.... Plaintiffs appeal from judgment entered on a jury verdict returned against them and in favor of the defendant.

The evidence shows that on the afternoon of April 25, 1967, defendant was driving his 1959 Chevrolet home from work; at the same time plaintiff Maxine Hammontree was working in a bicycle shop owned and operated by her and her husband; without warning defendant's car crashed through the wall of the shop, struck Maxine and caused personal injuries and damages to the shop.

Defendant claimed he became unconscious during an epileptic seizure losing control of his car. He did not recall the accident but his last recollection before it, was leaving a stop light after his last stop, and his first recollection after the accident was being taken out of his car in plaintiffs' shop. Defendant testified he has a medical history of epilepsy and knows of no other reason for his loss of consciousness except an epileptic seizure; prior to 1952 he had been examined by several neurologists whose conclusion was that the condition could be controlled and who placed him on medication; in 1952 he suffered a seizure while fishing; several days later he went to Dr. Benson Hyatt who diagnosed his condition as petit mal seizure and kept him on the same medication; thereafter he saw Dr. Hyatt every six months and then on a yearly basis several years prior to 1967; in 1953 he had another seizure, was told he was an epileptic and continued his medication; in 1954 Dr. Kershner prescribed dilantin and in 1955 Dr. Hyatt prescribed phelantin; from 1955 until the accident occurred (1967) defendant had used phelantin on a regular basis which controlled his condition; defendant has continued to take medication as prescribed by his physician and has done everything his doctors told him to do to avoid a seizure; he had no inkling or warning that he was about to have a seizure prior to the occurrence of the accident.

In 1955 or 1956 the department of motor vehicles was advised that defendant was an epileptic and placed him on probation under which every six months he had to report to the doctor who was required to advise it in writing of defendant's condition. In 1960 his probation was changed to a once-a-year report.

Dr. Hyatt testified that during the times he saw defendant, and according to his history, defendant "was doing normally" and that he continued to take phelantin; that "[t]he purpose of the [phelantin] would be to react on the nervous system in such a way that where, without the medication, I would say to raise the threshold so that he would not be as subject to these episodes without the medication, so as not to have the seizures. He would not be having the seizures with the medication as he would without the medication compared to taking medication"; in a seizure it would be impossible for a person to drive and control an automobile; he believed it was safe for defendant to drive.

Appellants' [argue that the trial court] committed prejudicial error in refusing to give their [proposed] jury instruction on absolute liability.[10]

Under the present state of the law found in appellate authorities beginning with *Waters v. Pacific Coast Dairy, Inc.*, 55 Cal. App. 131 P.2d 588 (driver rendered unconscious from sharp pain in left arm and shoulder) through *Ford v. Carew & English*, 200 P.2d 828 (fainting spells from strained heart muscles), *Zabunoff v. Walker*, 13 Cal. Rptr. 463 (sudden sneeze), and *Tannyhill v. Pacific Motor Trans. Co.*, 38 Cal. Rptr. 774 (heart attack), the trial judge properly refused the instruction. The foregoing cases generally hold that liability of a driver, suddenly stricken by an illness rendering him unconscious, for injury resulting from an accident occurring during that time rests on principles of negligence.

Appellants seek to have this court override the established law of this state which is dispositive of the issue before us as outmoded in today's social and economic structure, particularly in the light of the now recognized principles imposing liability upon the manufacturer, retailer and all distributive and vending elements and activities which bring a product to the consumer to his injury, on the basis of strict liability in tort.... [A number of] authorities hold that "A manufacturer (or retailer) is strictly liable in tort when an article he places on the market, knowing that it is to be used without inspection for defects, proves to have a defect that causes injury to a human being...." Drawing a parallel with these products liability cases, appellants argue, with some degree of logic, that only the driver affected by a physical condition which could suddenly render him unconscious and who is aware of that condition can anticipate the hazards and foresee the dangers involved in his operation of a motor vehicle, and that the liability of those who by reason of seizure or heart failure or some other physical condition lose the ability to safely operate and control a motor vehicle resulting in injury to an innocent person should be predicated on strict liability.

We decline to superimpose the absolute liability of products liability cases to drivers under the circumstances here. The theory on which those cases are predicated is that manufacturers, retailers and distributors of products are engaged in the business of distributing goods to the public and are an integral part of the over-all producing and marketing enterprise that should bear the cost of injuries from defective parts.... This policy hardly applies here and it is not enough to simply say, as do appellants, that the insurance carriers should be the ones to bear the cost of injuries to innocent victims on a strict liability [aka "absolute liability"] basis. In *Maloney v. Rath*, 445 P.2d 513, followed by *Clark v. Dziabas*, 71 Cal. Rptr. 901, 445 P.2d 517, appellant urged that defendant's violation of a safety provision (defective brakes) of the Vehicle Code makes the violator strictly liable for damages caused by the violation. While reversing the judgment for defendant upon another ground, the California Supreme Court refused to apply the doctrine of strict liability to automobile drivers. The situation involved two users of the highway but the problems of fixing responsibility under a system of strict liability are as complicated in the instant case as those in *Maloney v. Rath*, and could only create uncertainty in the area of its concern. As stated in *Maloney*: "To invoke a rule of strict liability on users of the streets and highways, however, without also establishing in substantial detail how the new rule should operate would only contribute confusion to the automobile accident problem. Settlement and claims adjustment procedures would become chaotic until the new rules were worked out on a case-by-case basis, and the hardships of delayed compensation would be seriously intensified. Only the Legislature, if it deems it wise to do so, can avoid such difficulties by enacting a comprehensive plan for the compensation of automobile accident victims in place of or in addition to the law of negligence."

The instruction tendered by appellants was properly refused for still another reason. Even assuming the merit of appellants' position under the facts of this case in which defendant knew he had a history of epilepsy, previously had suffered seizures and at the time of the accident was attempting to control the condition by medication, the instruction does not except from its ambit the driver who suddenly is stricken by an illness or physical condition which he had no reason whatever to anticipate and of which he had no prior knowledge.

The judgment is affirmed.

WOOD, P.J., and THOMPSON, J., concur.

PRACTICE BRIEFING
SHAPIRA V. UNION NATIONAL BANK

As explained in Chapter Two, courts make many statements about the law. Each case appears in your casebook because of how the court resolved one legal issue. If you focus only on the statements of law concerning that issue, your briefs will stay short. To help identify that issue, check your syllabus and the book's table of contents. The legal issue will always relate to the subject noted in those materials. Before reading the case below, note the sample table of contents and syllabus entries.

> **Class Syllabus:** The following case might appear in a section called, "After Testator Passes, Can She Influence the Actions of the Living?"
> **Casebook's Table of Contents:** The following case might appear in a section called, "Dead Hand: The Attempt to Control Property After Death."

Shapira v. Union National Bank, 315 N.E.2d 825
(Ohio Com. Pl. 1974)

This is an action for a declaratory judgment and the construction of the will of David Shapira, M.D., who died April 13, 1973, a resident of this county....

The portions of the will in controversy are as follows:

"Item VIII. All the rest, residue and remainder of my estate, real and personal, of every kind and description and wheresoever situated, which I may own or have the right to dispose of at the time of my decease, I give, devise and bequeath to my three (3) beloved children, to wit: Ruth Shapira Aharoni, of Tel Aviv, Israel, or wherever she may reside at the time of my death; to my son Daniel Jacob Shapira, and to my son Mark Benjamin Simon Shapira in equal shares, with the following qualifications:

"(b) My son Daniel Jacob Shapira should receive his share of the bequest only, if he is married at the time of my death to a Jewish girl whose both parents were Jewish. In the event that at the time of my death he is not married to a Jewish girl whose both parents were Jewish, then his share of this bequest should be kept by my executor for a period of not longer than seven (7) years and if my said son Daniel Jacob gets married within the seven year period to a Jewish girl whose both parents were Jewish, my executor is hereby instructed to turn over his share of my bequest to him. In the event, however, that my said son Daniel Jacob is unmarried within the seven (7) years after my death to a Jewish girl whose both parents were Jewish, or if he is married to a non Jewish girl, then his share of my estate, as provided in item 8 above should go to The State of Israel, absolutely."

The provision for the testator's other son Mark, is conditioned substantially similarly. Daniel Jacob Shapira, the plaintiff, alleges that the condition upon his inheritance is unconstitutional, contrary to public policy and unenforceable because of its unreasonableness, and that he should be given his bequest free of the restriction. Daniel is 21 years of age, unmarried and a student at Youngstown State University....

CONSTITUTIONALITY

Plaintiff's argument that the condition in question violates constitutional safeguards is based upon the premise that the right to marry is protected by the Fourteenth Amendment to the Constitution of the United States....

In the case at bar, this court is not being asked to enforce any restriction upon Daniel Jacob Shapira's constitutional right to marry. Rather, this court is being asked to enforce the testator's restriction upon his son's inheritance. If the facts and circumstances of this case were such that the aid of this court were sought to enjoin Daniel's marrying a non-Jewish girl, then the doctrine of *Shelley v. Kraemer* would be applicable, but not, it is believed, upon the facts as they are....

Basically, the right to receive property by will is a creature of the law, and is not a natural right or one guaranteed or protected by either the Ohio or the United States constitution.... It is a fundamental rule of law in Ohio that a testator may legally entirely disinherit his children.... This would seem to demonstrate that, from a constitutional standpoint, a testator may restrict a child's inheritance. The court concludes, therefore, that the upholding and enforcement of the provisions of Dr. Shapira's will conditioning the bequests to his sons upon their marrying Jewish girls does not offend the Constitution of Ohio or of the United States....

PUBLIC POLICY

The condition that Daniel's share should be 'turned over to him if he should marry a Jewish girl whose both parents were Jewish' constitutes a partial restraint upon marriage. If the condition were that the beneficiary not marry anyone, the restraint would be general or total, and, at least in the case of a first marriage, would be held to be contrary to public policy and void. A partial restraint of marriage which imposes only reasonable restrictions is valid, and not contrary to public policy.... The great weight of authority in the

United States is that gifts conditioned upon the beneficiary's marrying within a particular religious class or faith are reasonable....

Plaintiff contends, however, that in Ohio a condition such as the one in this case is void as against the public policy of this state. In Ohio, as elsewhere, a testator may not attach a condition to a gift which is in violation of public policy.... There can be no question about the soundness of plaintiff's position that the public policy of Ohio favors freedom of religion and that it is guaranteed by Section 7, Article I of the Ohio Constitution, providing that "all men have a natural and indefeasible right to worship Almighty God according to the dictates of their own conscience." Plaintiff's position that the free choice of religious practice cannot be circumscribed or controlled by contract is substantiated by *Hackett v. Hackett*, 150 N.E.2d 431 (C.A. Lucas 1958). This case held that a covenant in a separation agreement, incorporated in a divorce decree, that the mother would rear a daughter in the Roman Catholic faith was unenforceable. However, the controversial condition in the case at bar is a partial restraint upon marriage and not a covenant to restrain the freedom of religious practice; and, of course, this court is not being asked to hold the plaintiff in contempt for failing to marry a Jewish girl of Jewish parentage....

It is noted, furthermore, in this connection, that the courts of Pennsylvania distinguish between testamentary gifts conditioned upon the religious faith of the beneficiary and those conditioned upon marriage to persons of a particular religious faith. In *In re Clayton's Estate*, the court upheld a gift of a life estate conditioned upon the beneficiary's not marrying a woman of the Catholic faith. In its opinion the court distinguishes the earlier case of *Drace v. Klinedinst*, 275 Pa. 266 (1922), in which a life estate willed to grandchildren, provided they remained faithful to a particular religion, was held to violate the public policy of Pennsylvania. In Clayton's Estate, the court said that the condition concerning marriage did not affect the faith of the beneficiary, and that the condition, operating only on the choice of a wife, was too remote to be regarded as coercive of religious faith....

The only cases cited by plaintiff's counsel in accord with the [Plaintiff's argument] are some English cases and one American decision. In England the courts have held that partial restrictions upon marriage to persons not of the Jewish faith, or of Jewish parentage, were not contrary to public policy or invalid. Other cases in England, however, have invalidated forfeitures of similarly conditioned provisions for children upon the basis of uncertainty or indefiniteness.... [A] later English case has upheld a condition precedent that a granddaughter-beneficiary marry a person of Jewish faith and the child of Jewish parents. The court distinguished the cases cited above as not applicable to a condition precedent under which the legatee must qualify for the gift by marrying as specified, and there was found to be no difficulty with indefiniteness where the legatee married unquestionably outside the Jewish faith....

The American case cited by plaintiff is that of *Maddox v. Maddox*. The testator in this case willed a remainder to his niece if she remain a member of the Society of Friends. When the niece arrived at a marriageable age there were but five or six unmarried men of the society in the neighborhood in which she lived. She married a non-member and thus lost her own membership. The court held the condition to be an unreasonable restraint upon marriage and void.... It can be seen that while the court considered the testamentary condition to be a restraint upon marriage, it was primarily one in restraint of religious faith. The court said that with the small number of eligible bachelors in the area the condition would have operated as a virtual prohibition of the niece's marrying, and that she could not be expected to 'go abroad' in search of a helpmate or to be subjected to the chance of being sought after by a stranger. The court distinguished the facts of its case from those in England upholding conditions upon marriage by observing that England was 'already overstocked with inhabitants' while this country had 'an unbounded extent of territory, a large portion of which is yet unsettled, and in which increase of population is one of the main elements of national prosperity....'

In arguing for the applicability of the *Maddox v. Maddox* test of reasonableness to the case at bar, counsel for the plaintiff asserts that the number of eligible Jewish females in this county would be an extremely small minority of the total population especially as compared with the comparatively much greater number in New York, whence have come many of the cases comprising the weight of authority upholding the validity of such clauses. There are no census figures in evidence. While this court could probably take judicial notice of the fact that the Jewish community is a minor, though important segment of our total local population, nevertheless the court is by no means justified in judicial knowledge that there is an insufficient number of eligible young ladies of Jewish parentage in this area from which Daniel would have a reasonable latitude of choice. And of course, Daniel is not at all confined in his choice to residents of this county, which is a very different circumstance in this day of travel by plane and freeway and communication by telephone, from the horse and buggy days of the 1854 *Maddox v. Maddox* decision. Consequently, the decision does not appear to be an appropriate yardstick of reasonableness under modern living conditions.

Plaintiff's counsel contends that the Shapira will falls within the principle of *Fineman v. Central National Bank*, 175 N.E.2d 837 (1961), holding that the public policy of Ohio does not countenance a bequest or device conditioned on the beneficiary's obtaining a separation or divorce from his wife. Counsel argues that the Shapira condition would encourage the beneficiary to marry a qualified girl just to receive the bequest, and then to divorce her afterward. This possibility seems too remote to be a pertinent application of the policy against bequests conditioned upon divorce....

Finally, counsel urges that the Shapira condition tends to pressure Daniel, by the reward of money, to marry within seven years without opportunity for mature reflection, and jeopardizes his college education. It seems to the court, on the contrary, that the seven year time limit would be a most reasonable grace period, and one which would give the son ample opportunity for exhaustive reflection and fulfillment of the condition without constraint or oppression. Daniel is no more being 'blackmailed into a marriage by immediate financial gain,' as suggested by counsel, than would be the beneficiary of a living gift or conveyance upon consideration of a future marriage-an arrangement which has long been sanctioned by the courts of this state.

In the opinion of this court, the provision made by the testator for the benefit of the State of Israel upon breach or failure of the condition is most significant for two reasons. First, it distinguishes this case from... *Maddox v. Maddox*..., and, in a way, from the vagueness and indefiniteness doctrine of some of the English cases. Second, and of greater importance, it demonstrates the depth of the testator's conviction. His purpose was not merely a negative one designed to punish his son for not carrying out his wishes. His unmistakable testamentary plan was that his possessions be used to encourage the preservation of the Jewish faith and blood, hopefully through his sons, but, if not, then through the State of Israel. Whether this judgment was wise is not for this court to determine. But it is the duty of this court to honor the testator's intention within the limitations of law and of public policy. The prerogative granted to a testator by the laws of this state to dispose of his estate according to his conscience is entitled to as much judicial protection and enforcement as the prerogative of a beneficiary to receive an inheritance.

It is the conclusion of this court that public policy should not, and does not preclude the fulfillment of Dr. Shapira's purpose, and that in accordance with the weight of authority in this country, the conditions contained in his will are reasonable restrictions upon marriage, and valid.

PRACTICE BRIEFING
DODGE V. FORD MOTOR COMPANY

Dodge v. Ford Motor Company is more complicated than the cases in Appendices A and B. It's a lengthy decision with a detail-filled fact pattern, and the court spends many pages reviewing the plaintiff's and defendant's arguments. As you brief the case, don't get caught up in the minutia within the facts; instead, focus on the theme of the facts, or the big picture. Also, don't confuse the court's review and rejection of the plaintiff's and defendant's arguments with the court's holding and rationale. Whenever you read a case, especially a complicated one, look for language that the court uses to flag the issue and holding.

If you want a small hint for this case, I can tell you exactly what language to look for. (Skip right to the case if you don't want any spoilers.) After reviewing the facts, and then analyzing and rejecting a number of arguments, the court writes, "The case for plaintiffs must rest upon the [following] claim...." With this language, the court tells you: *Here is the issue.* The court goes on to write, "The rule which will govern courts in deciding these questions is not in dispute...." Now the court tells you: *Here is the rule we use to reason about this issue.* Once the court applies the rule to the issue, you will know the holding and rationale. So with those two sentences, the court tells you where to find the key components of your brief. Look for that language as a beacon while you read this case. Once you're done with your brief, compare your work to the brief following the case.

* * *

Class Syllabus: The following case might appear in a section called, "Corporations Exist for the Benefit of Shareholders."
Casebook's Table of Contents: The following case might appear in a section called, "Corporate Interests Other Than Maximizing Shareholder Wealth."

Dodge v. Ford Motor Company, 204 Mich. 459, 170 N.W. 668 (Mich. 1919)

Appeal from Circuit Court.... Action by John F. Dodge and Horace E. Dodge against the Ford Motor Company and others. Decree for plaintiffs, and defendants appeal. Affirmed in part and reversed in part.

The Ford Motor Company is a corporation, organized and existing under Act No. 232 of the Public Acts of 1903.... Section 2 of the act relates, in part, to the articles of association, and what shall appear in them, and the fourth subdivision of this section reads: ".... the amount of the total authorized capital stock which shall not be less than one thousand dollars, and not more than twenty-five million dollars...."

In 1917 (Pub. Acts 1917, No. 254), the maximum of capital stock was fixed at $50,000,000.

The second clause of the ninth subdivision of the same section reads, in part, as follows:

The amount of the capital stock and number of shares of every corporation organized under this act may be increased or diminished at any annual meeting of the stockholders, or at a special meeting expressly called for that purpose, by a vote of two-thirds of the capital stock of the corporation.

Section 14 reads:

> Every such corporation shall have power to purchase, hold and convey all such real and personal estate as the purposes of the corporation shall require.... Any corporation formed under this act may purchase real or personal property necessary for its business...; and in the absence of actual fraud in the transaction, the judgment of the directors as to the value of the property shall be conclusive. And in addition to the powers hereinbefore enumerated, every corporation organized under this act shall possess and exercise all such rights and powers as are necessarily incidental to the exercise of the powers expressly granted herein. It may also purchase and hold any grant of land made by the government to aid in any work of internal improvement....

Article II of the articles of association reads:

> The purpose or purposes of [Ford Motor Company] are as follows: To purchase, manufacture and placing on the market for sale of automobiles or the purchase, manufacture and placing on the market for sale of motors and of devices and appliances incident to their construction and operation.

> The parties... who signed the articles, included Henry Ford..., John F. Dodge, Horace E. Dodge, the plaintiffs, Horace H. Rackham and James Couzens,... and several other persons. The company began business in the month of June, 1903. In the year 1908, its articles were amended and the capital stock increased from $150,000 to $2,000,000....
>
> The business of the company continued to expand. The cars it manufactured met a public demand, and were profitably marketed, so that, in addition to regular quarterly dividends equal to 5 percent monthly on the capital stock of $2,000,000, its board of directors declared and the company paid special dividends: [dates and

amounts of special dividends omitted.] Sales and profits for several years were: Year ending Sept. 30, 1910, 18,664 cars, $4,521,509.51. Year ending Sept. 30, 1911, 34,466 cars, $6,275,031.07. Year ending Sept. 30, 1912, 68,544 cars, $13,057,312.24. Year ending Sept. 30, 1913, 168,304 cars, $25,046,767.43. Year ending Sept. 30, 1914, 248,307 cars, $30,338,454.63. Ten months ending July 31, 1915, 264,351 cars, $24,641,423.17. Three years ending July 31, 1916, 472,350 cars, $59,994,918.01.

The surplus above capital stock was, September 30, 1912, $14,745,095.67, and was increased year by year to $28,124,173.68, $48,827,032.07,$59,135,770.66.July 31,1916,it was $111,960,907.53. Originally, the car made by the Ford Motor Company sold for more than $900. From time to time, the selling price was lowered and the car itself improved until in the year ending July 31, 1916, it sold for $440. Up to July 31, 1916, it had sold 1,272,986 cars at a profit of $173,895,416.06. As the cars in use multiplied, sales of parts and or repairs increased, so that, in the year ending July 31, 1916, the gross profits from repairs and parts was $3,915,778.94; sales being more than $600,000 for each of the months of May, June, and July. For the year beginning August 1, 1916, the price of the car was reduced $80 to $360....

From a mere assembling plant, the plant of the Ford Motor Company came to be a manufacturing plant, in which it made many of the parts of the car which in the beginning it had purchased from others. At no time has it been able to meet the demand for its cars or in a large way to enter upon the manufacture of motor trucks.

No special dividend having been paid after October, 1915 (a special dividend of $2,000,000 was declared in November, 1916, before the filing of the answers), the plaintiffs, who together own 2,000 shares, or one-tenth of the entire capital stock of the Ford Motor Company, on the 2d of November, 1916, filed in the circuit court for the county of Wayne, in chancery, their bill of complaint..., in which bill they charge that since 1914 they have not been represented on the board of directors of the Ford Motor Company, and that since that time the policy of the board of directors has been dominated and controlled absolutely by Henry Ford, the president of the company, who owns and for several years has owned 58 percent of the entire capital stock of the company;.... Setting up that on the 31st of July, 1916, the end of its last fiscal year, the said Henry Ford gave out for publication a statement of the financial condition of the company..., that for a number of years a regular dividend, payable quarterly, equal to 5 percent monthly upon the authorized capital stock, and the special dividends hereinbefore referred to, had been paid, it is charged that notwithstanding the earnings for the fiscal year ending July 31, 1916, the Ford Motor Company has not since that date declared any special dividends:

> And the said Henry Ford, president of the company, has declared it to be the settled policy of the company not to pay in the future any special dividends, but to put back into the business for the future all of the earnings of the company, other than the regular dividend of five percent monthly upon the authorized capital stock of the company—two million dollars ($2,000,000).

This declaration of the future policy, it is charged in the bill, was published in the public press in the city of Detroit and throughout the United States in substantially the following language: "My ambition," declared Mr. Ford, "is to employ still more men; to spread the benefits of this industrial system to the greatest possible number, to help them build up their lives and their homes. To do this, we are putting the greatest share of our profits back into the business."

It is charged further that the said Henry Ford stated to plaintiffs personally, in substance, that as all the stockholders had received back in dividends more than they had invested they were not entitled to receive anything additional to the regular dividend of 5 percent a month, and that it was not his policy to have larger dividends declared in the future, and that the profits and earnings of the company would be put back into the business for the purpose of extending its operations and increasing the number of its employees, and that, inasmuch as the profits were to be represented by investment in plants and capital investment, the stockholders would have no right to complain. It is charged (paragraph 16) that the said Henry Ford,

> dominating and controlling the policy of said company, has declared it to be his purpose—and he has actually engaged in negotiations looking to carrying such purposes into effect—to invest millions of dollars of the company's money in the purchase of iron ore mines...; to acquire by purchase or have built ships for the purpose of transporting such ore to smelters to be erected...; and to construct and install steel manufacturing plants to produce steel products to be used in the manufacture of cars at the factory of said company; and by this means to deprive the stockholders of the company of the fair and reasonable returns upon their investment by way of dividends to be declared upon their stockholding interest in said company.

Setting up that the present invested assets of the company, exclusive of cash on hand, as of July 31, 1916, represented more than 30 times the present authorized capital of the company, and 2 1/2 times the maximum limit ($25,000,000) fixed by the laws of the state of Michigan for capitalization of such companies (now $50,000,000), it is charged that the present investment in capital and assets constitutes an unlawful investment of the earnings, and that the continued investment of earnings would be a continuation of such unlawful policy. Setting up unsuccessful efforts to secure a conference with Mr. Ford for the purpose of discussing the question and asking that there be a distribution of a part of the accumulations, it is charged: That on September 28, 1916, plaintiffs addressed to him, and had delivered to him by registered letter, the following communication:

> We have for some time, as you know, been endeavoring to make an appointment to see you, for the purpose—as you assumed and informed one of your associates—of discussing

the affairs of the Ford Motor Company from the standpoint of our interest as stockholders and with a view to securing action by the board of directors looking to a very substantial distribution from its cash surplus as dividends.

Not having been able to make an appointment to discuss the matter with you personally, as we very much desired to do, we write you this letter upon the subject.

The conditions shown by your recent financial statement — showing approximately $60,000,000 of net profits for the past year and cash surplus in bank exceeding $50,000,000 — it seems to us would suggest, without the action being requested, the propriety of the board taking prompt action to distribute a large part of the accumulated cash surplus as dividends to the stockholders to whom it belongs.

While we would be sorry to have any controversy over the matter, we feel that your attitude toward the stockholders of the company is entirely unwarranted.

The statements that you have made — that the stockholders are and have been receiving as dividends all they are entitled to — shows a most extraordinary state of mind if it represents your real feelings.

While a dividend of five percent per month, sixty percent per annum, on the capital stock of the company, $2,000,000, on its face would seem to be a large dividend — the fact is, however, that the assets of the company representing its surplus is as much the property of the stockholders as the assets representing the capital stock and the stockholders are as much entitled to a dividend that will give them returns on their surplus investment as their capital stock.

Looking at the situation in this way, the dividend being paid the stockholders is only a little above one percent on their capital employed in the business and entirely out of proportion to what the stockholders are entitled to.

In view of the existing circumstances, we ask that you promptly call a meeting of the board of directors to consider the situation and lay before them our views as stockholders as outlined in this letter, and we desire to say in this connection that we conceive it to be the duty of the board of directors to distribute as a minimum a special dividend of not less than fifty percent of the accumulated cash surplus of the company.

Another matter that we desire brought to the attention of the board is our contention as stockholders—that the company has no right to use the company's earnings in the continued extension of the plants and property of the company—indeed, from our point of view, they have already exceeded their authority in this direction.

We would be pleased to have your acknowledgment of the receipt of this letter and advise that you have called a meeting of the board of directors for the purpose of considering and acting upon the matters referred to in it.

And that they sent on the same day copies to each of the members of the board of directors of the Ford Motor Company, and one to Edsel B. Ford, secretary. That, although the said Henry Ford and each of the directors were in the city of Detroit at the time of the receipt of such communication, no attention was paid to it and no acknowledgment made by said Henry Ford personally, but in his behalf his son, Edsel, under date October 10, 1916, replied:

I beg to acknowledge due receipt of your letter of September 23, 1916, and to say that it would have been answered before this but for my absence from town for a considerable length of time and pressure of other matters.

It seems to me, in view of all the conditions of business and our extensions, which have been determined upon for so long a time past and to which we have been working, that it would not be wise to increase the dividends at the present time—but, nevertheless, I will lay your letter before the board of directors and we will give your views regarding the increase of dividends and extensions full consideration at our next meeting.

Plaintiffs addressed another letter to Mr. Ford, dated October 11th, acknowledging the receipt of the communication of October 10th, and containing, among other things, the following:

> Rumors are current to the effect that the company has very ambitious plans for the expansion of the operations of the company under consideration and negotiations looking to carrying them into effect that would involve the disbursement of a large part of the cash assets of the company.
>
> We would thank you very much to advise us by early mail as to whether there is any foundation for the rumors referred to and that plans for the extension or expansion of the operations of business of the company that would absorb any considerable part of the company's present resources, are under consideration and the status of any negotiations relating thereto. In short, as stockholders, we would ask to be advised promptly as to what plans for the enlargement of the plants, property or operations are under way or under consideration.
>
> Of course, it would be idle to have the board of directors consider the question of disbursing the cash assets of the company in dividends, if, before the board has considered our request, the same have been appropriated in the directions referred to.
>
> We would respectfully urge that we be given a prompt and full reply to this letter.

And it is charged that up to the date of filing the bill no reply had been received or acknowledgment of said communication. Paragraphs 25, 26, 27, and 28 of the bill read:

> (25) That during the year ending July 31, 1916, the output of the said Ford Company's product amounted to approximately five hundred thousand (500,000) automobiles—yielding to the company, as stated, a net profit of sixty million dollars ($60,000,000). That although there was no reason to

conclude that said company could not repeat its production of 500,000 cars during the succeeding year and sell the
same readily at the price at which they had been sold in the
previous year, and although labor and material costs were
increasing, the said Henry Ford forced upon the board of
directors his policy of reducing the price of such cars by
eighty dollars ($80) per car, making a difference in the net
sales price of the product of said company for the year ending July 31, 1917, of forty million dollars ($40,000,000).
That such policy was adopted only for the purpose of
enabling him to continue to carry out the policy he had
decided upon to extend the operations and increase the
said company's output of manufactured automobiles and
a production schedule for the year July 31, 1916, to July
31, 1917, for eight hundred thousand (800,000) cars was
adopted. That in order to prepare for such increased production the company is now, in carrying out such policy of said Henry Ford, engaged in practically duplicating
the enormous plant of the company at Highland Park in
the county of Wayne and state of Michigan, and in making other large expenditures and preparing to make other expenditures involving millions of dollars in carrying
out such plan of the expansion of the business plants and
property of the company.

(26) That unless restrained by the injunction of this honorable
court, the said Henry Ford will cause the cash assets that
would otherwise be available for dividends, to be disbursed
and invested in fixed capital assets.

(27) In the face of the increased labor and material cost and
the uncertain conditions that will prevail in the business
world at the termination of the present world war, the policy of said Henry Ford, in continuing the expansion of the
business of said corporation, is reckless in the extreme and
seriously jeopardizes the interest of your orators as stockholders in said corporation.

(28) That there are many other corporations engaged in the business of manufacturing cars in competition with the only car manufactured by the Ford Motor Company, to wit, the class recognized in the trade as "low-priced cars." That the annual production of such other companies of such class of cars runs into the hundreds of thousands of cars per annum. That if the said Henry Ford is permitted to continue the policy that he has inaugurated and announced he is determined to carry out, of increasing production, reducing the price of cars, and increasing the capital investments in the conduct of such business by withholding the dividends from stockholders to which they are entitled, the necessary result will be the destruction of competition on the sale of the class of ears manufactured by such corporation and the creation of a complete monopoly in the manufacture and sale of such cars in violation of the state, federal and common law.

Paragraphs 30 and 31 read:

(30) That by reason of the declared policy of said Henry Ford not to pay dividends and to continue the expansion of the business of said company, including the risks involved in various enterprises proposed to be carried on by said company, your orators' interest in said Ford Motor Company which is worth not less than $50,000,000, is practically limited to a valuation fixed by the dividends so regularly to be declared, which, as stated, amount to little more than one percent upon the actual capital investment of the stockholders of the company in the business of said corporation and renders the disposition of your orators' stockholding interest in said corporation, except at a sacrifice, impossible.

(31) That the operations of said corporation should by the injunction of this honorable court, be limited at least to the conduct of the company's business within the limits of its

present capital investment, not including its cash accumulations, and your orators' interests as such stockholders
should not be put in jeopardy by the reckless ventures proposed to be entered upon in connection with the carrying
out of the policy of expansion of the said Henry Ford as
above herein outlined.

Plaintiffs ask for an injunction to restrain the carrying out of
the alleged declared policy of Mr. Ford and the company, for a decree requiring the distribution to stockholders of at least 75 percent
of the accumulated cash surplus, and for the future that they be
required to distribute all of the earnings of the company except
such as may be reasonably required for emergency purposes in the
conduct of the business.

The answer of the Ford Motor Company, which was filed November 28, 1916, admits most of the allegations in the plaintiffs'
bill of complaint.... It denies that Henry Ford forced upon the
board of directors his policy of reducing the price of cars by $80,
and says that the action of the board in that behalf was unanimous
and made after careful consideration. It admits that it has decided
to increase the output of the company and is engaged in practically
duplicating its plan at Highland Park; that plans therefor have been
under consideration and practically agreed upon for a year and the
lands necessary for the expansion acquired a year before this suit
was begun and their acquisition laid before the board on the 28th
of January, 1916, and ratified; that these plans were made public
as early as December, 1915; and, upon information and belief, it
is alleged that the plaintiffs knew all about it and never made any
complaint until they filed their bill in this cause, unless the letter
set forth in the bill of complaint can be called a complaint; that it
has been the policy of the company and its practice for eight or ten
years to cut the price of cars and increase the output, a plan which
has been productive of great prosperity, and that what was done the
1st of August, 1916, was strictly in accordance with this policy; that
it was not carried out by cutting the price of cars August 1, 1915,

because after full discussion it was determined that the proposed expansions of business were necessary to secure the continued success of the company and that a considerable additional sum ought to be accumulated for the purpose of extensions and making the improvements complained of; that this policy for the year ending July 31, 1916, was understood by all the directors and the management and, it is believed, by all of the stockholders, including the plaintiffs; that the expansion is well under way, building operations are being carried on; that there is a great demand for Ford trucks which could not be supplied without such expansion; that only such extensions and expansions are contemplated as are shown in the estimates found in the minutes of the directors' meeting. It is denied that the proposed expansions jeopardize the interests of the plaintiffs and asserted that they are in accordance with the best interests of the company and in pursuance of their past policy. It is denied that the policy continued would destroy competition, and any idea of creating a monopoly is denied. The allegations in regard to mining, shipping, and transporting iron ore are denied, or that anything is being done or contemplated which will result in disaster. Any plan or purpose or thought to injure or impair the value of plaintiffs' capital stock is denied, while it is asserted that their interests will be improved. The minutes attached to this answer showing action of the board of directors at meetings held in October and November, 1916, are voluminous. They show, among other things, approval of a purchase of property in the city of New York costing $560,052.40. They show discussion of plans regarding a building to be erected on such property, and deferred action. They show that various purchases of property made during the year 1916, from May to August, in Chicago, Detroit, Kansas City, New Jersey, Cleveland, Ohio, Iowa, costing upwards of $900,000, were ratified, and an assembly plant ordered to be constructed at Des Moines, Iowa, at approximately the cost of $420,000. The minutes of the meeting of the board of directors, held November 2, 1916, after providing for the purchase of certain lands adjacent to the plant of the defendant company, contain the following:

Whereas, the officers have proceeded with the preparations for the increase of the plant and have started the erection of some of the buildings to that end, and having incurred expenditures in connection therewith, the details of which have been laid before the board and duly considered, together with approximate estimates of the total cost of such extensions with explanations by the officers and engineers of this company....

Now, therefore, resolved that the proceedings and action heretofore taken and the expenditures made in the works aforesaid be hereby ratified and confirmed; and further resolved, that the officers are authorized to proceed with such plans for building extensions, purchase of equipment, tools and fixtures as in their judgment most advantageous and economical for this company....

And, with respect to certain new operations, contain the following:

The adoption of the following resolution was moved by Mr. Couzens and supported by Mr. Rackham:

Whereas this company has for some time past been making preparations looking to the manufacture of its own iron and the erection of a manufacturing plant on lands to be acquired from Mr. Henry Ford at the River Rouge, Wayne county, Michigan, for that purpose, and whereas approximate estimates have been submitted by the company's engineers for such work...

And whereas, certain steps have been taken by the management preliminary to such work, including the hiring of an engineer, preparation of plans, etc.

Now, therefore, resolved that the undertaking aforesaid be proceeded with, that the action heretofore taken in that behalf be ratified and confirmed and the officers and management are authorized to go forward with said works as in their judgment may be most advantageous and economical to this company and they are authorized to execute and carry out necessary contracts in connection with such work and make all payments required in the course thereof.

And resolved, that this company purchase of Henry Ford for the purposes aforesaid [lands] at the cost thereof to Mr. Ford with interest at the rate of 6 percent per annum, approximately $700,000 and the officers are instructed to accept conveyances from Mr. Ford and to pay the price stated upon transfer being completed, and

Resolved further, that the expense of turning basin and dredging of the canal, as shown upon the plans of the engineers, half of such canal being upon the lands of Mr. Ford and half upon the lands of this company, be borne equally by this company and by Mr. Ford, and that the management be authorized to proceed with such work and make the necessary arrangements to divide the expense.

Carried unanimously.

A further resolution was offered to build a building on property owned by the company in New York City for offices and salesroom and to lease the balance of the building for hotel purposes; the building to cost approximately $740,000. At the directors' meeting held November 8, 1916, a dividend of 100 percent on the capital stock was ordered paid, and the resolution with respect to the hotel building in New York City carried. At a meeting of directors held November 13, 1916, the following resolution was unanimously adopted:

It was moved, supported and unanimously carried that in view of written reports of Engineers Mayo and Kennedy (hereto attached) and the oral report of the president of the company, that all things considered, it seems more desirable to locate the proposed blast furnaces, steel plant and other extensions on the location on River Rouge, rather than on the Detroit river, and that the officers of the company are hereby authorized to proceed with the preparations for such extensions and acquiring of the land as originally passed at the directors' meeting of November 2, 1916, but that no new contracts be entered into until the injunction against the directors has been disposed of.

The answer of Henry Ford is a repetition in many respects of the matter contained in the answer of the Ford Motor Company. He denies that he has declared it to be the settled policy of the company not to pay any special dividends but to put back into the business for the future all the earnings of the company other than the regular dividends of 5 percent monthly. He denies that he made a declaration as to his future policy as controlling stockholder in fixing the policy for the management of the corporation. He admits that he used the language substantially set out in the 13th paragraph of the bill, hereinbefore set out, and he does not deny, but admits, that his ambition is as therein stated, but that his action as a director will be controlled by future conditions and with due respect to the interests of all concerned. He declares that he has been and always is open to argument and conviction as to what is best and what is right in the conduct of the affairs of the Ford Motor Company. He denies that he stated personally to plaintiffs in substance that as all of the stockholders had received back in dividends more than they had invested they were not entitled to receive anything additional to the regular dividend of 5 percent per month, and that it was not his policy to have larger dividends declared in the future, and that the proceeds and earnings of the company would be put back into the business, etc. He denies the allegations of the sixteenth subdivision of the bill, and specifically:

> Defendant denies that he has declared it to be his purpose to invest millions of dollars of the company's money in the purchase of iron ore mines anywhere or to acquire by purchase or have built ships for the purpose of transporting ore. He admits that he caused an investigation to be made relative to obtaining the necessary ore for the proposed blast furnaces hereinafter referred to, but upon having such investigation

made several months ago he found that there was abundant competition in the iron ore market and that it was wholly unnecessary and undesirable to acquire ore in any other way than by purchase, and therefore all thought in that direction was abandoned. The same is true with respect to the acquisition of ships for the transportation of ore. This defendant says that the Ford Motor Company has for more than a year past been laying plans publicly and openly for the building of blast furnaces, stoves, blowing engines, coke ovens, foundry buildings and equipment, malleable foundries and equipment and the necessary accompaniments therefor, for the purpose of producing the iron used in the construction of the cars of the Ford Motor Company. That some contracts have been entered into by the company to that end and some substantial amounts paid out upon the preliminary work. He shows that such blast furnaces and the works above described will be for the great benefit and advantage of the company, not only in the direct saving of cost of iron parts, but in the improvement of the quality thereof. He further shows that the present plans do not contemplate the manufacture of steel but that in the future it is hoped to be able to produce at comparatively small increased expense the steel required by the Ford Motor Company in the manufacture of its cars. This defendant denies absolutely the allegation... that this defendant proposed to deprive the stockholders of the company of the fair and reasonable return upon their investments.

He answers the charges in the bill respecting attempts on the part of plaintiffs to have an interview with him, explaining why a desired interview did not take place, says he supposed that the proposed interview related to a desire on the part of plaintiffs to sell their stock in the Ford Motor Company to him as they had previously attempted to do. He admits the receipt of letters referred to in the bill of complaint. He admits that the letter of October 11th, written by the plaintiffs, was not answered until on or about

November 3d, but he denies that in the meantime he continued to carry out plans to disburse the cash of the company so that there would not be funds available for declaring dividends.

The twenty-fifth paragraph of the answer is as follows:

25. This defendant denies that he forced upon the board of directors his policy of reducing the price of such cars by eighty dollars per car and says that the action of the board was unanimous thereon after careful consideration. This defendant admits that it was decided to increase the output of the company and admits that the company is engaged in practically duplicating the plant at Highland Park. He shows that the plans therefor have been under discussion and have been adopted for practically a year past and that the entire organization has been working to that end. He shows that most of the lands necessary for such expansion for the Highland Park plant were acquired nearly a year ago. That the plans had been made public as early as last December, and upon information and belief he shows that the plaintiffs knew all about it and that they never made any complaint with respect to it until the time of filing the bill herein, unless the letters referred to in the bill, written by the plaintiffs, could be said to be such complaint. This defendant shows that it has been the practice of the Ford Motor Company for the past eight or ten years to cut the price of the car annually and to increase the output. That such policy has been productive of great prosperity to the company and to its stockholders. That what was done in that regard on the 1st of August, 1916, was strictly in pursuance of the regular policy of the company. That this policy of cutting the price was not carried out on the 1st of August, 1915, because in the counsels of the company, among its active managers it was, after full discussion, decided that the proposed expansion and buildings were necessary to the continued success of the company and that it would be wiser and better not to cut the price during

the fiscal year ending July 31, 1916, in order that a considerable additional fund might be accumulated for the very purpose of building the extensions and making the improvements that are now being complained of by the plaintiffs. This policy so adopted for the fiscal year ending July 31, 1916, was thoroughly understood by all the directors and active members of the management and as this defendant is informed and believes by all of the stockholders, including the plaintiffs. Original price of the touring car which is now sold at three hundred and sixty dollars was upwards of nine hundred dollars, being substantially the same car although it has been greatly improved in many respects since the time when it was sold at nine hundred dollars and upwards. The cuts in the price have been made substantially every year except for the fiscal year ending July 31, 1916. This defendant has every reason to believe that the action of the board of directors in reducing the price for the current year was very wise and this defendant denies that it was adopted for any reason except the permanent good of the company. This defendant admits that construction is now under way and has been for months past in increasing and practically duplicating the size of the plant at Highland Park. Much of the machinery for such expansion has heretofore been ordered, the exact particulars of which will be furnished to the court. This defendant was not present at the meeting of the board of November 2d. He is informed that the reason why the appropriation for the large building referred to in the estimate was not passed was that construction could not commence until the opening of spring. Building extension is now approaching completion. The Ford Motor Company is now far behind its orders. The expansion is absolutely essential for the continued prosperity and success of the corporation. There is a great demand for Ford trucks, but the manufacturing department of the company has been unable to supply the demand and is now utterly unable to meet the demand. It is estimated by the manufacturing department that it cannot turn out to exceed ten thousand trucks this year, whereas it is the estimate of the sales department that one hundred thousand could be sold if they could be turned out.

Paragraph 27 of the answer reads:

27. This defendant denies that proposed expansion is reckless or that it threatens to jeopardize the interest of the plaintiff but shows that the same is strictly in accordance with the best interests of the company and its stockholders and strictly in pursuance of the past policy of the company. That the proposed expansion and extension are practical, feasible and have only been decided upon after the most careful investigation and advice of experts of the highest obtainable capacity.

Paragraph 36 reads:

36. Further answering this defendant shows that personally he has always been in favor of maintaining very large cash balances; that he has always been opposed to borrowing money and that he has urged the policy of paying cash for extensions and expansions and other expenses; that he has often in the past yielded his better judgment in the extent of dividends to be paid after discussion with other members of the board; that some of the large dividends paid have been against this defendant's better judgment, but after discussing it he has yielded his judgment to the other members of the board who at the present time are practically the same as during all the past successful years of the corporation, although Mr. John F. Dodge, who was a member for a number of years retired on or about the 18th day of August, 1913. This defendant shows that he has no fixed and unalterable views on the subject of dividends, but is always ready and willing to discuss with other members of the board what seems to be right under the circumstances. Inasmuch as the company was contemplating the entering

upon large enterprises of expansion involving large amounts of cash, this defendant has insisted upon great caution in the matter of dividends, particularly in view of the conditions of business throughout the world. This defendant shows that the expenditures of the Ford Motor Company from day to day are very great and its requirements of cash are enormous. He shows that if, by any chance, there should be a sudden falling off of business or collapse of business that it would require great sums of money to carry on the business of the company, and his idea is to be well fortified against emergencies. This defendant is opposed to any policy which would necessitate the discharge of large number of employees in case there should be a sudden depression of business if there be any way to avoid it, and this defendant believes that the latter methods and policies ultimately redound to the best financial interests of the company and its stockholders. This defendant is not in favor of paying out in dividends the surplus of the company to the danger point or any point where it could be regarded as risky in the least degree. This defendant further shows that he is not in favor of keeping up the price of the car to the highest possible point that the public will apparently stand for the time being, but he is in favor of the policy of reducing the price of the car from time to time as the safety and welfare of the company and stockholders will dictate, since he believes such to be a better, permanent policy for the company. Such always has been the policy adopted in the past, and he believes that such has been one of the causes of the unexampled success of the company....

All of the answers had been filed on November 28th, and were used in a showing, in opposition to plaintiffs' application for an injunction, an order to show cause and a restraining order having been made November 2d. The motion for injunction came on to be heard November 29th, in the circuit court for the county of Wayne, in chancery; three circuit judges sitting. An opinion upon the application for a temporary injunction was filed December 9, 1916. The conclusions of two of said judges are expressed in the following excerpt from the opinion:

> We are of the opinion that the expansion of the business, by way of the establishment of a smelting plant, at the River Rouge, should be restrained, pending an early hearing upon the question of whether the diverting of accumulated cash profits to that end is an abuse of discretion on the part of the directors. This involves a mixed question of fact and law, and we feel that the allegations of the bill, and the showing in support thereof, makes this a question to be decided only on a hearing upon the merits, and therefore matters should stand as they are, pending such hearing.
>
> Considering the importance of the questions involved, we feel there should be a hearing on the merits within 60 days. Let an injunction issue restraining defendants from using accumulated cash profits on hand for the establishment of a smelting plant.

The third judge concurred in granting the injunction, but refused to concur in the conclusion that the defendant corporation could lawfully engage in the smelting business. An order having been entered in the circuit court in accordance with the opinion, application was made to the Supreme Court for a writ of mandamus to vacate and set aside said order. Upon that application, it appearing that considerable contracts had been made, that loss would attend an interruption of the carrying out of plans, and that Mr. Ford and others had offered to indemnify the company and plaintiffs, an alternative order was issued, whereupon the order for temporary injunction was modified in such way as to permit the use of the accumulated cash profits of the Ford Motor Company not exceeding $10,000,000 for the establishment of a smelting plant during the pendency of this suit and until the further order of the court, upon condition that a bond in the sum of $10,000,000, conditioned to refund to the Ford Motor Company all money so used, be given, and also conditioned that such obligation may be enforced against such defendants by the final decree herein or by supplemental proceedings in this cause. Thereupon Messrs. Ford, Rackham, and Klingensmith made their writing obligatory in accordance with said order, and the bond was approved January 6, 1917.

The cause came on for hearing in open court on the 21st of May, 1917. A large volume of testimony was taken, with the result that a decree was entered December 5, 1917, in and by which it is decreed that within 30 days from the entry thereof the directors of the Ford Motor Company declare a dividend upon all of the shares of stock in an amount equivalent to one-half of, and payable out of, the accumulated cash surplus of said Ford Motor Company, on hand at the close of the fiscal year ending July 31, 1916, less the aggregate amount of the special dividends declared and paid after the filing of the bill and during the year ending July 31, 1917; the amount to be declared being $19,275,385.96. It was further decreed:

Third. The owning, holding or operating by the defendant, Ford Motor Company, of, and the using or appropriating or incurring obligations which might require or necessitate the using or appropriating of any funds or other property of said defendant, Ford Motor Company, for a smelting plant or blast furnace or furnaces of the kind or character which the proofs adduced herein show to be contemplated and now in course of construction on or near the River Rouge, and of any lands, buildings, machinery or equipment therefor, and other incident thereof, is without authority of law and is permanently and absolutely restrained and enjoined.

Fourth. The increase of the fixed capital assets of the defendant, Ford Motor Company, beyond those at the date of the entry hereof owned and held by the said corporation, is without authority of law and is permanently and absolutely restrained and enjoined. The date of the entry hereof is taken, instead of the date of the objections raised by plaintiffs to any such increase, at the suggestion of plaintiffs, so that said corporation shall not be in any wise embarrassed through the wrongful acts of the individual defendants. The said fixed capital assets so owned and held at the date of the entry hereof shall be deemed to include such further investment as may be necessary to complete or to complement the same so as to be properly usable in the conduct of the regular business of the said corporation. The said fixed capital assets shall be deemed to be exclusive of those of the kind or character contemplated in the next preceding paragraph hereof.

The holding of liquid assets (including accumulations of and from the earnings and profits of regular business operations from time to time) by the defendant, Ford Motor Company, in excess of such as may be reasonably required in the proper conduct and carrying on of the business and operations of said corporation in connection with, and by the use of, the fixed capital assets, limited as aforesaid, is likewise without authority of law and is permanently and absolutely restrained and enjoined, and said defendant corporation and its board of directors, the individual defendants herein and their respective successors in office, are directed and commanded to declare and distribute, as dividends to the stockholders, any such excess which may now exist or may accrue from time to time hereafter. The term 'liquid assets' as used herein shall be deemed to include all assets other than fixed capital assets within the meaning generally understood in business of said last mentioned term.

The intent and purpose of this subdivision 'fourth' of this decree is to fix a maximum limit for the aggregate assets of the defendant, Ford Motor Company, and if it be practicable to increase either class (fixed or liquid) of assets out of the other without affecting the aggregate, such increase shall be proper — the limit in this subdivision stated for each class having been adopted as the most convenient manner of stating the limit of the aggregate.

The defendants Ford, Rackham, and Klingensmith are ordered to account for any and all sums used since the filing of the bill in and about the establishment of a smelting plant, and within 30 days after the accounting is completed to pay to the Ford Motor Company, in pursuance of the obligation of the undertaking executed by them, the amount by such accounting found and determined to have been in fact paid out in and about the work aforesaid, and to discharge all liabilities incurred in that behalf, taking from the Ford Motor Company conveyance and transfer of any and all property purchased and acquired in the establishment of said plant. Dates are fixed for the payment of the special dividend ordered to be made, and plaintiffs are awarded their costs....

Defendants have appealed, plaintiffs have not appealed, from the decree. In the briefs, appellants state and discuss the following propositions:

(1) The claim of plaintiffs' counsel that a manufacturing corporation in Michigan may not have more than twenty-five million (now fifty million) of capital assets, is without merit.

(2) Monopoly. There is nothing in the antitrust laws which affects this case. Mere bigness of a corporation is not unlawful.

(3) It is lawful for the Ford Motor Company to build blast furnaces at the Rouge.

   (a) No claim in this regard is made by plaintiffs in the bill of complaint.

   (b) The plaintiffs are estopped by their conduct to raise the question.

   (c) The work is not ultra vires the corporation.

(4) The management of the corporation and its affairs rests in the board of directors, and no court will interfere or substitute its judgment so long as the proposed actions are not ultra vires or fraudulent. They may be ill advised, in the opinion of the court, but this is no ground for exercise of jurisdiction.

(5) The board has full power over the matter of investing the surplus and as to dividends so long as they act in good faith.

(6) Such rights of management and control over investments and dividends are not only rules of law, they are rights fixed by the contract between the parties in the formation of the corporation.

(7) These things are so although the majority of the stock is held by one man. It is the right and the duty of the majority to control. This duty must be exercised, and the responsibility cannot be shifted or evaded.

(8) Motives of the board members are not material and will not be inquired into by the court so long as the acts are within their lawful powers.

(9) Motives of a humanitarian character will not invalidate or form the basis of any relief so long as the acts are within the lawful powers of the board, if believed to be for the permanent welfare of the company.

(10) The court will not entertain a bill to enforce unconscionable demands, no matter what the legal rights of plaintiffs may be.

In the brief for plaintiffs, the grounds for relief are stated as follows:

(1) The proposed scheme of expansion is not for the financial advantage of the corporation, either mediate or immediate, and is not to be prosecuted with that intent, but for the purpose of increasing the number of employees and of the cars produced, to the end of giving employment and low-priced cars to a greater number of people.

> (These are ends worthy in themselves but not within the scope of an ordinary business corporation — ends which, if prosecuted, should be by individuals associated for such purposes.)

(2) If the proposed scheme of expansion were for the proper and legitimate uses and needs of the corporation and a

cash surplus equivalent to that accumulated and now on hand were necessary for the business of the corporation, nevertheless, a proper dividend ought to be required to be declared and paid out of such accumulated cash surplus, because the only reason there would not be ample cash on hand for all purposes, including proper dividends, is that the price of the cars and of the parts therefor, has been arbitrarily fixed at a figure which it is intended shall not produce a net profit sufficient to fulfill all those requirements, including the payment of proper dividends, and the requiring of the payment of dividends will force, and it is the only way by which can be forced the fixing of prices which will produce the requisite amount of net profits.

> (The whole scheme is to bring about such a relation of wages, revenue and cash requirements of the business as to preclude dividends of a reasonable return upon the fair value of the capital stock.)

(3) The relation, irrespective of any limitation imposed by statute, between the authorized capital stock of the Ford Motor Company, $2,000,000.00, and the accumulated surplus (outside of cash on hand and municipal bonds in which some of the same has been temporarily invested), $58,000,000.00, is such as in and of itself requires the prevention of the further conversion of accumulated cash surplus from current earnings into capital investment against the objection of any stockholder.

(4) A smelting plant for the manufacture from the ore of iron for use in the manufacture of automobiles is not within the power of a corporation organized under Act 232 of the Public Acts of 1903.

(5) The capital stock of a corporation organized under Act 232 of the Public Acts of 1903 is limited to $25,000,000.00, and as defendant corporation has now, as shown by the financial statement, an actual capital investment (outside of cash

on hand and municipal bonds in which some of the same has been temporarily invested) of $60,000,000.00, the conversion of the accumulated cash surplus from current earnings into capital investment by the enlargement of the plant and facilities for the manufacture and sale of automobiles is within the inhibition of the statutory limitation.

1. *Argued before [judges] OSTRANDER, C. J., and BIRD, MOORE, STEERE, BROOKE, FELLOWS, STONE, and KUHN, JJ.*

Lucking, Helfman, Lucking & Hanlon, of Detroit (Alfred Lucking, Alexis C. Angell, L. B. Robertson, Horace H. Rackham, and Hubert E. Hartman, all of Detroit, of counsel), for appellants.

Stevenson, Carpenter, Butzel & Backus, of Detroit (Elliott G. Stevenson, William L. Carpenter, and Thomas G. Long, all of Detroit, of counsel), for appellees.

2. *[Legal analysis by Judge] OSTRANDER, C. J. (after stating the facts as above).*

The authorized capital stock of the defendant company is $2,000,000. Its capital, in July, 1916, invested in some form of property, including accounts receivable, was $78,278,418.65, and, less liabilities other than capital stock, was more than $60,000,000. Besides this, it had and was using as capital nearly $54,000,000 in cash or the equivalent of cash. It is contended by plaintiffs that because the statute has prescribed that the total authorized capital stock shall be not less than $1,000, and not more than $25,000,000 (now $50,000,000), the capital of any corporation organized under the act may not lawfully exceed $25,000,000 (now $50,000,000). In the argument presented by them the term 'capital' is used as meaning:

The aggregate of the sums subscribed and paid in or secured to be paid in by the shareholders, with the addition of all gains or profits realized in the use and investment of those sums; or, if losses have been incurred, then it is the residue after deducting such losses.

Pointing out that the shares of stock are at all times representative of the capital, whatever it may be, it is said that the learned trial judge decided that:

> It was the legislative intent to prohibit a corporation having a capital in excess of the maximum limitation, whether that excess was acquired by contributions from stockholders or from profits on those contributions.

And, in the judgment of counsel for plaintiffs, the essence of the reasoning employed by the trial judge may be... stated by them in this language:

> Looking at the statute, the history of the times, and the constitutional provision respecting corporations, it appears that the limitation in question was put in the statute because it was believed that mischief would result unless a restriction was placed upon corporate capital; that it was the intent of the statute to prevent this mischief; that to permit corporations to increase their capital, at pleasure, from undivided profits, would frustrate that intent and give to old corporations powers, rights, and privileges which were not given to new corporations, and thus make corporations unequal before the law, contrary to the intent of the provision in our Constitution respecting corporations to place them all on a basis of equality.

It was the opinion of the three judges to whom was presented the application for a temporary restraining order that the statute, in the language referred to, does not limit the amount of capital — that portion of the assets of a corporation regardless of their source, utilized for the conduct of the corporate business for the purpose of deriving gains and profits — which a corporation organized under the act may lawfully possess.

The term "capital stock," in its primary sense, means the fund, property, or other means contributed or agreed to be contributed by shareholders as the financial basis for the prosecution of the business of the corporation, being made directly through stock subscriptions or indirectly through the declaration of stock dividends. The capital stock of a corporation is always representative of the net assets of the corporation, whatever they may be.... The section of the statute with which we are dealing relates to the organization of corporations, and, plainly, it is the legislative intent that no more than $50,000,000 of capital shall be, in the first instance, aggregated and embarked in business under this law. It has been the policy of the state, unlike that of most of the states, to limit the aggregate of capital which, in the first instance, may be employed in corporate enterprises; but the history of legislation is not evidence of a continuing state policy which limits the capital assets of corporations. Act No. 41, Public Acts of 1853, authorized the formation of manufacturing corporations. It contained the provision:

> The amount of the capital stock in every such corporation shall be fixed and limited by the stockholders in their articles of association, and shall, in no case, be less than ten thousand dollars, nor more than five hundred thousand dollars, and shall be divided into shares of twenty-five dollars each. The capital stock may be increased, and the number of shares, at any meeting of the stockholders called for that purpose: Provided, that the amount so increased shall not, with the existing capital, exceed five hundred thousand dollars.

In 1875, Act No. 89, this law was amended.... The express terms are that, subject to [certain omitted] limitations, the capital stock may be increased or diminished, etc. In argument, significance is attached to the language employed in the act of 1853 authorizing an increase of capital stock, but providing that the amount of the increase "with the existing capital" shall not exceed the maximum of $500,000. Significance is also attached to the language in the amending acts which permit an increase of capital stock subject to the limitations as to minimum and maximum of capital stock.

Assuming that the Legislature in passing the law of 1853 had in view the distinction between capital stock and capital, or capital assets, and intended a maximum limitation of the amount of capital, the assumption must, of course, rest upon the language employed in the law. When the Legislature in the latter act omitted the words upon which the assumption is based, no reason is apparent for the conclusion that the limitation of capital was still intended. If the act of 1853 contains evidence of a policy limiting capital assets, the act of 1903 contains no such evidence.

There is no apparent reason for entering upon the task of interpreting or construing language which is self-interpreting, which has a clear, reasonable meaning. The same general implications are to be drawn from the phrase "not more than," as from the phrase "not less than." We are not called upon to find a reason for the policy of limiting the capital stock or for the failure to also limit the value of the assets which may at any time be employed in the corporate business. We may assume a legislative reason, but may not assume that, because a possible reason may be given for a further limitation, such further limitation must be implied.

The reasons given for a different interpretation of the language, reasons which introduce matter not in the statute, are inconclusive. If the claimed statute limitation exists, it is imperative. It is manifestly impracticable, if not impossible, to limit the use in its business by a corporation, of any size, of its profits, to require that, when organized with the maximum amount of capital stock, all profits shall be set aside. It is conceded, in argument, that there must be some variation, some leeway. But, if any, how much? It may be supposed that the Legislature looked with disfavor upon an initial aggregation of capital exceeding a certain amount. It cannot be supposed that it looked with disfavor upon a profitable corporate existence.

Subscriptions to capital stock may be paid for in property valued by those associating. It may be that a patent is contributed which, until exploited, has only an estimated potential value—no selling value—but, after exploitation, would sell for more than the maximum limit fixed for capital stock. No one would contend that a $50,000,000 manufacturing corporation could not borrow money for the purpose of its business. Of course, if it borrowed, it would owe for the money and, as matter of bookkeeping, would not by borrowing expand its capital assets. But, in fact, at the expense of a small rate of interest, it might add $50,000,000 to the capital actually employed in business.

Experience would not lead to the belief that any manufacturing corporation, of any size, would continue to embark in the enterprise such profits as competition permitted and stockholders were willing to forego, to the public detriment. It happens that the Ford Motor Company has had an unusual, a phenomenal, experience; but this affords no reason for finding the meaning in the statute which plaintiffs insist shall be given to it. That no limit is in terms placed upon the value of assets—capital—which may be employed is a circumstance supporting the conclusion that none was intended.

Any aggregation of capital, from $1,000 to $50,000,000, is now permitted—invited—to be embarked in business under this statute, the corporations formed to compete among themselves, and with foreign corporations admitted to do business in this state. The purpose of any organization under the law is earnings—profit. Undistributed profits belong to the corporation, and, so far as any limitation can be found in this act, may be lawfully employed as capital. If the meaning of the law were more doubtful, it would be prudent, if not imperative, that the Legislature be left to make plain what is supposed to be obscure.

There is little, if anything, in the bill of complaint which suggests the contention that the smelting of iron ore as a part of the process of manufacturing motors is, or will be, an activity ultra vires the defendant corporation. On the contrary, the bill charges that the erection of smelters and such other buildings, machinery, and appliances as are intended to go along with the business of smelting ore, is part of a general plan of expansion of the business of defendant corporation which is in itself unwise and which is put into operation for the purpose of absorbing profits which ought to be distributed to shareholders. Restraint is asked, not because the smelting business is ultra vires the corporation, but because the whole plan of expansion is inimical to shareholders' rights and was formulated and will be carried out in defiance of those rights.

The gray iron parts of a Ford car weigh, in the rough, 268.90 pounds, and when finished 215.71 pounds. This iron, as now made by defendants, costs per car, at the prices of iron when the cause was tried, $11.184. The malleable iron parts weigh, finished, per car, 69.63 pounds, and would cost $6.757. The total cost per car of gray and malleable iron parts is less than $18.

The smelter proposition involves, of course, much more than the initial expenditure for a plant. It involves the use of a large amount of capital to secure the finished product for the cars. Quantities of iron ore must be purchased and carried in stock; coal for the coke ovens must be purchased; the plant must be maintained. If the plant produces the necessary iron, and 800,00 cars are made in a year, something more than 270,000,000 pounds of iron ore will be produced, and if, as is claimed by Mr. Ford, the cost is reduced to the company by one-half and better iron made, a saving of $9 or $10 on the cost of each car will be the result. Presumably, this saving will also be reflected in the profits made from sales of parts. Ultimately, the result will be, either a considerable additional profit upon each car sold, or it will permit a reduction in the selling price of cars and parts. The process proposed to be used has not been used commercially.

The contention that the project is ultra vires the defendant corporation appears to have been made upon the application for a preliminary restraining order, and at the hearing on the merits, as a reason for denying the right to invest instead of distributing the money which the proposed plant will cost, with no claim of surprise upon the part of defendants.

Strictly, upon the pleadings, the question of ultra vires is not for decision, and this is not seriously denied. Assuming, however, in view of the course taken at the hearing, it is proper to express an opinion upon the point, it must be said that to make castings from iron ore, rather than to make them from pig iron, as defendant is now doing, eliminating one usual process, is not beyond the power of the corporation. In its relation to the finished product, iron ore, an article of commerce, is not very different from lumber. It is admitted that the defendant company may not undertake to smelt ore except for its own uses. Defendant corporation is organized to manufacture motors and automobiles and their parts. To manufacture implies the use of means of manufacturing as well as the material. No good reason is perceived for saying that as matter of power it may not manufacture all of an automobile. In doing so, it need not rely upon the statute grant of incidental powers. Extreme cases may be put; as, for example, if it may make castings from iron ore, may it invest in mines which produce the ore and in means for transporting the ore from mine to factory? Or, if it may make the rubber tires for cars, may it own and exploit a rubber plantation in Brazil, or elsewhere? No such case is presented, and until presented need not be considered.

As we regard the testimony as failing to prove any violation of anti-trust laws or that the alleged policy of the company, if successfully carried out, will involve a monopoly other than such as accrues to a concern which makes what the public demands and sells it at a price which the public regards as cheap or reasonable, the case for plaintiffs must rest upon the claim, and the proof in support of it, that the proposed expansion of the business of the corporation, involving the further use of profits as capital, ought to be enjoined because inimical to the best interests of the company and its shareholders, and upon the further claim that in any event the withholding of the special dividend asked for by plaintiffs is arbitrary action of the directors requiring judicial interference.

The rule which will govern courts in deciding these questions is not in dispute. It is, of course, differently phrased by judges and by authors, and, as the phrasing in a particular instance may seem to lean for or against the exercise of the right of judicial interference with the actions of corporate directors, the context, or the facts before the court, must be considered. This court, in Hunter v. Roberts, Throp & Co., 83 Mich. 63, 71, 47 N. W. 131, 134, recognized the rule in the following language:

> It is a well-recognized principle of law that the directors of a corporation, and they alone, have the power to declare a dividend of the earnings of the corporation, and to determine its amount.... Courts of equity will not interfere in the management of the directors unless it is clearly made to appear that they are guilty of fraud or misappropriation of the corporate funds, or refuse to declare a dividend when the corporation has a surplus of net profits which it can, without detriment to its business, divide among its stockholders, and when a refusal to do so would amount to such an abuse of discretion as would constitute a fraud, or breach of that good faith which they are bound to exercise towards the stockholders.

In Cook on Corporations (7th Ed.) § 545, it is expressed as follows:

> The board of directors declare the dividends, and it is for the directors, and not the stockholders, to determine whether or not a dividend shall be declared.
>
> When, therefore, the directors have exercised this discretion and refused to declare a dividend, there will be no interference by the courts with their decision, unless they are guilty of a willful abuse of their discretionary powers, or of bad faith or of a neglect of duty. It requires a very strong case to induce a court of equity to order the directors to declare a dividend, inasmuch as equity has no jurisdiction, unless fraud or a breach of trust is involved. There have been many attempts to sustain such a suit, yet, although the courts do not disclaim jurisdiction, they have quite uniformly refused to interfere. The discretion of the directors will not be interfered with by the courts, unless there has been bad faith, willful neglect, or abuse of discretion.
>
> Accordingly, the directors may, in the fair exercise of their discretion, invest profits to extend and develop the business,

and a reasonable use of the profits to provide additional facilities for the business cannot be objected to or enjoined by the stockholders.

In Morawetz on Corporations (2d Ed.) § 447, it is stated:

Profits earned by a corporation may be divided among its shareholders, but it is not a violation of the charter if they are allowed to accumulate and remain invested in the company's business. The managing agents of a corporation are impliedly invested with a discretionary power with regard to the time and manner of distributing its profits. They may apply profits in payment of floating or funded debts, or in development of the company's business; and so long as they do not abuse their discretionary powers, or violate the company's charter, the courts cannot interfere.

But it is clear that the agents of a corporation, and even the majority, cannot arbitrarily withhold profits earned by the company, or apply them to any use which is not authorized by the company's charter. The nominal capital of a company does not necessarily limit the scope of its operations; a corporation may borrow money for the purpose of enlarging its business, and in many instances it may use profits for the same purpose. But the amount of the capital contributed by the shareholders is an important element in determining the limit beyond which the company's business cannot be extended by the investment of profits. If a corporation is formed with a capital of $100,000 in order to carry on a certain business, no one would hesitate to say that it would be a departure from the intention of the founders to withhold profits, in order to develop the company's business, until the sum of $500,000 had been amassed, unless the company was formed mainly for the purpose of accumulating the profits from year to year. The question in each case depends upon the use to which the capital is put and the meaning of the company's charter. If a majority of the shareholders or the directors of a corporation wrongfully refuse to declare a dividend and distribute profits earned by the company, any shareholder feeling aggrieved may obtain relief in a court of equity.

It may often be reasonable to withhold part of the earnings of a corporation in order to increase its surplus fund, when it would not be reasonable to withhold all the earnings for that purpose. The shareholders forming an ordinary business corporation expect to obtain the profits of their investment in the form of regular dividends. To withhold the entire profits merely to enlarge the capacity of the company's business would defeat their just expectations. After the business of a corporation has been brought to a prosperous condition, and necessary provision has been made for future prosperity, a reasonable share of the profits should be applied in the payment of regular dividends, though a part may be reserved to increase the surplus and enlarge the business itself.

One other statement may be given from Park v. Grant Locomotive Works, 40 N. J. Eq. 114, 3 Atl. 162 (45 N. J. Eq. 244, 19 Atl. 621):

In cases where the power of the directors of a corporation is without limitation, and free from restraint, they are at liberty to exercise a very liberal discretion as to what disposition shall be made of the gains of the business of the corporation. Their power over them is absolute so long as they act in the exercise of their honest judgment. They may reserve of them whatever their judgment approves as necessary or judicious for repairs or improvements, and to meet contingencies, both present and prospective. And their determination in respect of these matters, if made in good faith and for honest ends, though the result may show that it was injudicious, is final, and not subject to judicial revision.

It is not necessary to multiply statements of the rule.

To develop the points now discussed, and to a considerable extent they may be developed together as a single point, it is necessary to refer with some particularity to the facts.

When plaintiffs made their complaint and demand for further dividends, the Ford Motor Company had concluded its most prosperous year of business. The demand for its cars at the price of the preceding year continued. It could make and could market in the year beginning August 1, 1916, more than 500,000 cars. Sales of parts and repairs would necessarily increase. The cost of materials was likely to advance, and perhaps the price of labor; but it reasonably might have expected a profit for the year of upwards of $60,000,000. It had assets of more than $132,000,000, a surplus of almost $112,000,000, and its cash on hand and municipal bonds were nearly $54,000,000. Its total liabilities, including capital stock, was a little over $20,000,000. It had declared no special dividend during the business year except the October, 1915, dividend. It had been the practice, under similar circumstances, to declare larger dividends. Considering only these facts, a refusal to declare and pay further dividends appears to be not an exercise of discretion on the part of the directors, but an arbitrary refusal to do what the circumstances required to be done. These facts and others call upon the directors to justify their action, or failure or refusal to act. In justification, the defendants have offered testimony tending to prove... the following facts: It had been the policy of the corporation for a considerable time to annually reduce the selling price of cars, while keeping up, or improving, their quality. As early as in June, 1915, a general plan for the expansion of the productive capacity of the concern by a practical duplication of its plant had been talked over by the executive officers and directors and agreed upon; not all of the details having been settled, and no formal action of directors having been taken. The erection of a smelter was considered, and engineering and other data in connection therewith secured. In consequence, it was determined not to reduce the selling price of cars for the year beginning August 1, 1915, but to maintain the price and to accumulate a large surplus to pay for the proposed expansion of plant and equipment, and perhaps to build a plant for smelting ore. It is hoped, by Mr. Ford, that eventually 1,000,000 cars will be annually produced. The contemplated changes will permit the increased output.

The plan, as affecting the profits of the business for the year beginning August 1, 1916, and thereafter, calls for a reduction in the selling price of the cars. It is true that this price might be at any time increased, but the plan called for the reduction in price of $80 a car. The capacity of the plant... would produce more than 600,000 cars annually. This number, and more, could have been sold for $440 instead of $360, a difference in the return for capital, labor, and materials employed of at least $48,000,000. In short, the plan does not call for and is not intended to produce immediately a more profitable business, but a less profitable one; not only less profitable than formerly, but less profitable than it is admitted it might be made. The apparent immediate effect will be to diminish the value of shares and the returns to shareholders.

It is the contention of plaintiffs that the apparent effect of the plan is intended to be the continued and continuing effect of it, and that it is deliberately proposed, not of record and not by official corporate declaration, but nevertheless proposed, to continue the corporation henceforth as a semi-eleemosynary institution and not as a business institution. In support of this contention, they point to the attitude and to the expressions of Mr. Henry Ford.

Mr. Henry Ford is the dominant force in the business of the Ford Motor Company. No plan of operations could be adopted unless he consented, and no board of directors can be elected whom he does not favor. One of the directors of the company has no stock. One share was assigned to him to qualify him for the position, but it is not claimed that he owns it. A business, one of the largest in the world, and one of the most profitable, has been built up. It employs many men, at good pay.

"My ambition," said Mr. Ford, "is to employ still more men, to spread the benefits of this industrial system to the greatest possible number, to help them build up their lives and their homes. To do this we are putting the greatest share of our profits back in the business."

With regard to dividends, the company paid sixty percent on its capitalization of two million dollars, or $1,200,000, leaving $58,000,000 to reinvest for the growth of the company. This is Mr. Ford's policy at present, and it is understood that the other stockholders cheerfully accede to this plan.

He had made up his mind in the summer of 1916 that no dividends other than the regular dividends should be paid, "for the present."...

The record, and especially the testimony of Mr. Ford, convinces that he has to some extent the attitude towards shareholders of one who has dispensed and distributed to them large gains and that they should be content to take what he chooses to give. His testimony creates the impression, also, that he thinks the Ford Motor Company has made too much money, has had too large profits, and that, although large profits might be still earned, a sharing of them with the public, by reducing the price of the output of the company, ought to be undertaken. We have no doubt that certain sentiments, philanthropic and altruistic, creditable to Mr. Ford, had large influence in determining the policy to be pursued by the Ford Motor Company—the policy which has been herein referred to.

It is said by his counsel that—

Although a manufacturing corporation cannot engage in humanitarian works as its principal business, the fact that it is organized for profit does not prevent the existence of implied powers to carry on with humanitarian motives such charitable works as are incidental to the main business of the corporation.

And again:

As the expenditures complained of are being made in an expansion of the business which the company is organized to carry on, and for purposes within the powers of the corporation as hereinbefore shown, the question is as to whether such expenditures are rendered illegal because influenced to some extent by humanitarian motives and purposes on the part of the members of the board of directors.

In discussing this proposition, counsel have referred to [a number of cases]. These cases... like all others in which the subject is treated, turn finally upon the point, the question, whether it appears that the directors were not acting for the best interests of the corporation. We do not draw in question, nor do counsel for the plaintiffs do so, the validity of the general proposition stated by counsel nor the soundness of the opinions delivered in the cases cited. The case presented here is not like any of them. The difference between an incidental humanitarian expenditure of corporate funds for the benefit of the employees, like the building of a hospital for their use and the employment of agencies for the betterment of their condition, and a general purpose and plan to benefit mankind at the expense of others, is obvious. There should be no confusion (of which there is evidence) of the duties which Mr. Ford conceives that he and the stockholders owe to the general public and the duties which in law he and his codirectors owe to protesting, minority stockholders. A business corporation is organized and carried on primarily for the profit of the stockholders. The powers of the directors are to be employed for that end. The discretion of directors is to be exercised in the choice of means to attain that end and does not extend to a change in the end itself, to the reduction of profits, or to the nondistribution of profits among stockholders in order to devote them to other purposes.

There is committed to the discretion of directors, a discretion to be exercised in good faith, the infinite details of business, including the wages which shall be paid to employees, the number of hours they shall work, the conditions under which labor shall be carried on, and the price for which products shall be offered to the public.

It is said by appellants that the motives of the board members are not material and will not be inquired into by the court so long as their acts are within their lawful powers. As we have pointed out, and the proposition does not require argument to sustain it, it is not within the lawful powers of a board of directors to shape and conduct the affairs of a corporation for the merely incidental benefit of shareholders and for the primary purpose of benefiting others, and no one will contend that, if the avowed purpose of the defendant directors was to sacrifice the interests of shareholders, it would not be the duty of the courts to interfere.

We are not, however, persuaded that we should interfere with the proposed expansion of the business of the Ford Motor Company. In view of the fact that the selling price of products may be increased at any time, the ultimate results of the larger business cannot be certainly estimated. The judges are not business experts. It is recognized that plans must often be made for a long future, for expected competition, for a continuing as well as an immediately profitable venture. The experience of the Ford Motor Company is evidence of capable management of its affairs. It may be noticed, incidentally, that it took from the public the money required for the execution of its plan, and that the very considerable salaries paid to Mr. Ford and to certain executive officers and employees were not diminished. We are not satisfied that the alleged motives of the directors, in so far as they are reflected in the conduct of the business, menace the interests of shareholders. It is enough to say, perhaps, that the court of equity is at all times open to complaining shareholders having a just grievance.

Assuming the general plan and policy of expansion and the details of it to have been sufficiently, formally, approved at the October and November, 1917, meetings of directors, and assuming further that the plan and policy and the details agreed upon were for the best ultimate interest of the company and therefore of its shareholders, what does it amount to in justification of a refusal to declare and pay a special dividend or dividends? The Ford Motor Company was able to estimate with nicety its income and profit. It could sell more cars than it could make. Having ascertained what it would cost to produce a car and to sell it, the profit upon each car depended upon the selling price. That being fixed, the yearly income and profit was determinable, and, within slight variations, was certain.

.... [I]f the total cost of proposed [expansion] had been immediately withdrawn in cash from the cash surplus (money and bonds) on hand August 1, 1916, there would have remained nearly $30,000,000.

Defendants say, and it is true, that a considerable cash balance must be at all times carried by such a concern. But, as has been stated, there was a large daily, weekly, monthly, receipt of cash. The output was practically continuous and was continuously, and within a few days, turned into cash. Moreover, the contemplated expenditures were not to be immediately made. The large sum appropriated for the smelter plant was payable over a considerable period of time. So that, without going further, it would appear that, accepting and approving the plan of the directors, it was their duty to distribute on or near the 1st of August, 1916, a very large sum of money to stockholders.

In reaching this conclusion, we do not ignore, but recognize, the validity of the proposition that plaintiffs have from the beginning profited by, if they have not lately, officially, participated in, the general policy of expansion pursued by this corporation. We do not lose sight of the fact that it had been, upon an occasion, agreeable to the plaintiffs to increase the capital stock to $100,000,000 by a stock dividend of $98,000,000. These things go only to answer other contentions now made by plaintiffs, and do not and cannot operate to estop them to demand proper dividends upon the stock they own. It is obvious that an annual dividend of 60 percent upon $2,000,000, or $1,200,000, is the equivalent of a very small dividend upon $100,000,000, or more.

The decree of the court below fixing and determining the specific amount to be distributed to stockholders is affirmed. In other respects, except as to the allowance of costs, the said decree is reversed. Plaintiffs will recover interest at 5 percent per annum upon their proportional share of said dividend from the date of the decree of the lower court. Appellants will tax the costs of their appeal, and two-thirds of the amount thereof will be paid by plaintiffs. No other costs are allowed.

* * *

Here is how you would brief this case:

Dodge v. Ford Motor Company (Michigan, 1919)

- **Facts:** Ford refused to pay a dividend to shareholders on its massive earnings. Instead, it planned to expand and altruistically lower the cost of cars. Minority shareholders moved to block the expansion and demand a dividend.
- **Issue:** Can a corporation refuse to pay a dividend to shareholders and instead expand its business and lower the price of its cars to benefit the public good?
- **Procedural Posture:** Lower court held for plaintiffs, stopped the expansion, and mandated payment of a dividend. Appeals court affirmed the dividend but reversed the decision that Ford can't expand.
- **Resolution:** Even after paying for the expansion, Ford would have enough cash to pay a large dividend to its shareholders.
- **Holding:** Corporations exist for the benefit of shareholders. Directors cannot operate a corporation for the benefit of the public good at the expense of shareholder earnings.
- **Rationale:** Expanding the company is a reasonable business decision that might benefit shareholders in the long run. Even after paying to expand, Ford has sufficient earnings to pay a large dividend to shareholders. Withholding the dividend is an abuse of discretion.